Praise for *Talking to Depression*

"This book recognizes the power of altruism in healing, and the capacities of a depressed person to herself be a healer for others. . . . Strauss not only suggests how we can be a good friend to one who is depressed, but she provides us instructions on *how* to be a good friend. [*Talking to Depression* is] a really important tool for knowing how to relate and how to connect when people in your life are struggling with depression."

—Jo Cohen Hamilton, Ph.D.

"*Talking to Depression* is a war chest of tools to aid our understanding of something that defies understanding unless one has experienced it firsthand. . . . In an ideal world [this book] would not be needed. The next best thing would be that it finds its way into every home and library. Perhaps, in the right hands, this book could save lives."

—Christine B. Smith, Ph.D., President of Survivors of Loved Ones' Suicides, Inc. (S.O.L.O.S.)

"Ms. Strauss has created a wonderfully helpful book for all of us. An excellent manual for the day-to-day interaction with the depressed person. This book would be a wonderful addition to anyone's library that unfortunately will get excellent use!"

—Peter A. Schwartz, M.D.

"It is an essential read for the layperson that does not understand the experience of depression and wants to help a friend or family member through it . . . practical ideas, common sense guidelines and clear explanations that can make a difference in the lives of those with depression."

—Marta C. Peck, Executive Director of the Mental Health Association of Reading, PA, and Berks County

P9-DMW-052

continued . . .

"This book is about what the person suffering from depression needs to hear and, even more importantly, about what that person should *not* hear. . . . Strauss doesn't just give the persons with depression a chance to get the daily support they need, she gives the people who love them a way to feel renewed in their own lives. I found it enlightening, inspiring, and enormously instructive."

> —Nancy Wolter Brooks, Speech pathologist, and health, rehabilitation, and social work professional

"This magical book . . . makes numerous practical, valuable, and doable suggestions. It shows family and friends how to make a difference. With this guide, we can help the people we know who are struggling with this disease, and we can help ourselves. I couldn't recommend this book more strongly."

> —Catherine M. Schultz, School Counselor, Reading High School

"I can't say enough about Claudia Strauss's *Talking to Depression*. This is definitely a guide that is needed. I've never seen anything that addresses friends and family in this way—and so thoroughly, so compassionately, yet so simply. What a contribution to the field!"

> —Michelle Hostetter, Psy.D., Clinical Psychologist

Talking
to
Depression

Simple Ways to Connect When
Someone in Your Life Is Depressed

CLAUDIA J. STRAUSS

WITH A FOREWORD BY MARTHA MANNING, PH.D.

NAL
BOOKS

New American Library

New American Library
Published by New American Library, a division of
Penguin Group (USA) Inc., 375 Hudson Street,
New York, New York 10014, U.S.A.
Penguin Books Ltd, 80 Strand,
London WC2R 0RL, England
Penguin Books Australia Ltd, 250 Camberwell Road,
Camberwell, Victoria 3124, Australia
Penguin Books Canada Ltd, 10 Alcorn Avenue,
Toronto, Ontario, Canada M4V 3B2
Penguin Books (N.Z.) Ltd, Cnr Rosedale and Airborne Roads,
Albany, Auckland 1310, New Zealand

Penguin Books Ltd, Registered Offices:
80 Strand, London WC2R 0RL, England

First published by New American Library,
a division of Penguin Group (USA) Inc.

First Printing, January 2004
10 9 8 7 6 5 4 3 2 1

 REGISTERED TRADEMARK—MARCA REGISTRADA

LIBRARY OF CONGRESS CATALOGING-IN-PUBLICATION DATA:

Strauss, Claudia J., 1952–
Talking to depression: simple ways to connect when someone in your life is depressed / by
Claudia J. Strauss.
p. ; cm.
ISBN 0-451-20986-9
1. Depression, Mental—Popular works. 2. Depressed persons—Family relationships.
[DNLM; 1. Depression—psychology. 2. Communication. 3. Depressive Disorder—psychology.
4. Interpersonal Relations. WM 171 S912t 2004]
I. Title.
RC537.S835 2004
616.85'27—dc22   2003016852

Set in Minion
Designed by Ginger Legato

Printed in the United States of America

I dedicate this book to you, the reader,
and to the person in your life who is suffering.
And to all of us who will be touched by depression at some
point in our lives, whether directly or indirectly.

This book addresses what to say and what not to say,
what to do and what not to do.

This book is not for therapists; it is for the rest of us—
untrained—doing the best we can to live our lives
and help those around us.

Acknowledgments

$\mathcal{M}$any, many people have come into my life over the years, and all of them have touched me in some way. In a very real sense, they have all contributed to this book. Because of what I've experienced directly and indirectly. Because of what I've shared, observed, learned, and felt.

And many people have been directly involved in the creation of this book. As early readers. As readers of its various incarnations. As fact checkers. As editors. As supporters.

They include doctors, counselors, and other professionals in the field. People who suffer from severe depression and those who struggle with bipolar disorder. Their family members and friends.

I can't mention all of them here. I am particularly grateful to Marilyn Weller, who brought both her knowledge of this subject and her editorial savvy to bear on an early draft. To Marta Peck (Executive Director, Mental Health Association of Reading and Berks County) and Michelle Adams Hostetter, Ph.D., for multiple readings. To Jim Levine, who supported the concept. To Claire Zion, who embraced the project. To Jennifer Jahner and

Laura Cifelli for their fresh look at later drafts, for their editorial suggestions and for shepherding it through the process. To Rose Hilliard, for staying on top of things, and for her cheerfulness and informed responsiveness.

I would especially like to thank Martha Manning for her close reading of the manuscript, the suggestions she made that have enhanced the helpfulness of this book, and her enthusiasm for what a layperson can bring.

Thanks to the American Association of Suicidology and also to Suicide Awareness/Voices of Education (SAVE) for permission to print their warning/danger signs of suicide.

Thanks to the Cleveland Archives for tracking down the source of George Szell's words and verifying their accuracy, and to Charles Seliger for so generously giving his time to help me do the same with Willem de Kooning's words.

And though I can't mention everyone, I would like to list these few more: Peter Schwartz, Nancy Brooks, Deirdre Brown, Catherine Schultz, Nancy Knoblauch, Karen Tomlinson, Jill Einstein, Jo Cohen Hamilton, Christine Smith, Andrea Rander, and Karen Muldrow. Your feedback, your support and, especially, your conviction that this would fill a hole that needed to be filled have kept me going so that this project could reach fruition.

Thank you for helping me help others.

On a more personal note, I would like to thank the people who surround me with their thoughtfulness and wrap me in warmth. Here, too, the list is long. So many family members and friends. I hope you know who you are. This book is a testament to all of you.

"Suffering belongs to no language."

✒ ADELIA PRADO

(TRANSLATED BY ELLEN WATSON)

Contents

Contents

Foreword

When someone says, "I'm depressed," it's often hard to know exactly what he means. On the one hand, many of us use the word every day as part of casual conversation. We use it to describe the way we *feel*—sad, down, discouraged, bummed out, or hopeless. I refer to this as "little d" depression. Almost every one of us knows what little d depression feels like. Usually it's a temporary emotion that is successfully vanquished by a happy event, or it fades with the passage of time and requires little support from anyone.

But there is another, more serious kind of depression that I call the "Big D." This kind of depression includes a *collection* of feelings, thoughts, behaviors and physical changes or, in the terminology of mental-health professionals, "symptoms." Depending on whether these symptoms are mild or severe, they can interfere significantly with many aspects of a person's life. They also become a concern for those family, friends, coworkers, and even acquaintances who look on in dismay, knowing that something is wrong but not knowing how to understand it or what to do about it. It is estimated that one in ten Americans suffers from some form of clinical depression.

A great deal of trouble results when we confuse little d with Big D depressions. It leads those of us who want to help to faulty assumptions about what a person suffering from clinical depression is going through when, in reality, we haven't got a clue. It may lead us to thinking we have the answers to make things better, the solutions that will surely help the sufferer "snap out of it," get back on track. The problem is that many of the things that are helpful in lifting the spirits of someone who is temporarily down or blue are not at all helpful to a person who is suffering from clinical depression. In fact, as Claudia Strauss discusses in the following pages, despite the best of intentions, sometimes our words or actions may actually *hurt* the sufferer, unwittingly widening the gap between the person dealing with depression and the people who care more about him or her.

HOW BAD IS IT?

Like many other illnesses, clinical depression can vary from *mild* to *severe*. In a respiratory illness, for example, it's important to differentiate between a simple case of the sniffles and a situation with a high fever and difficulty breathing. We follow the symptoms and the degree to which those symptoms interfere with normal living. It can also be important to know how long the person has been ill, whether the changes we notice came on slowly and gradually or with more of a "bang." This is very much the case with depression. We may know someone who has had the equivalent of the depression "sniffles" for a year. He is able to show up for the basics, but it is as if the color has drained from his life. In contrast, we may have a loved one who changed seemingly overnight from being a happy, productive, energetic person to one who is paralyzed in constant self-doubt, lost in sadness with frequent tears and expressing an alarming hopelessness about her life. One person is no more "deserving" of attention than another, but the onset of the problems as well as the degree to which they interfere with the sufferer's life may determine how quickly and strongly we intervene.

For the purposes of this book, it is less important to get caught up in all the fancy nomenclature that comes with medical illnesses. It is less important for us to be fluent in types and subtypes than to be comfortable "knowing the enemy" enough to help a loved one do battle with it. To get a good understanding of depression, it's critical to know what parts of a person's functioning take a hit: Which parts of their lives are compromised by this illness? And how does this show itself in everyday life? Depression is particularly tough on several integral parts of human functioning, which I will divide into the following categories:

Mood
Thinking
Behavior
Physical Changes

MOOD

When we think of depression, mood is often the first thing that comes to mind. Feelings and emotions are part of mood. People with depression suffer from low or negative mood that can range from seeming "less happy than usual" to persistently tearful and sad. They feel stuck and hopeless that things will ever change. Mood doesn't respond well to common sense or the reasons that are clear to everyone else about why a person should be happy. Just to make things more complicated, depression often "hangs out" with two particularly good friends—anxiety and irritability—which can make being with the friend or loved one just that much harder. The anxious person is sad, worried and difficult to comfort. The irritable person is easily, but often unpredictably, "set off," so that we see increased criticism and complaining. Since anxiety and irritability make the most "noise," it can be easy to overlook the depression at the root of the problem.

Sometimes a person's mood "reacts" and sometimes it doesn't. A joke, a happy child, an evening out for pizza may "boost" the sufferer. It's important to know the difference between them and those people for whom winning a million bucks in the lottery wouldn't bring a smile. With these people it's like an invisible wall exists between them and the world that they once found so exciting, loving, challenging and wonderful.

THINKING

Depression interferes with *what* and *how* we think. First, there's the content of our thoughts. Basically, depression sufferers see the world through dark-colored glasses. If they are going to agree with something, it will typically be a grudging, "Yes, but . . ." response, where they never wholeheartedly concede agreement. Negative thoughts tend to focus on the self, the world and the future. While the depression sufferer does not show the same degree of disturbances in reality testing as someone with schizophrenia, there is still distortion going on. "I have always been a failure." "Our marriage has never been good." "It's my fault my daughter's relationship with her boyfriend is so bad." "Nothing will change." "What's the point of trying?" Negative thinking can go from mild and somewhat open to other people's input to oppressively dark and hopeless in a way that responds to very little. Often, people who think this rigidly are at greater risk of attempting suicide and are in need of immediate professional intervention.

Depression poisons a person's thoughts in familiar ways: "Things stink." "They won't change." "I'm a bad person." "*You're* a bad person." This is sometimes referred to as "broken record" thinking, and whichever side of it you're on, it's easy to see why. But depression doesn't only sour people's attitudes about themselves and others. *Depression makes it harder to think.* And in some ways this is worse. Big D can make it difficult to remember, or to organize work or ideas that were once automatic. Car-pool commitments or volunteer events may go out the window because of what depression sufferers often call a "haze." They find themselves trying to "maintain" at work and home on cruise control, which only works for so long. Most frustratingly, sufferers may not be able to translate their thoughts and feelings as easily as they used to do with loved ones. It's as if the password for access has changed, but no one knows what it is, leaving everyone feeling frustrated and isolated. Reading, attending a play or concert, and other hobbies that make people feel good about themselves all require concentration that's gone missing, and may make people feel like strangers in their own lives. There is often an unexpressed fear about how much cognitive ability they will lose in the future. It is striking how many times people recovering from depression make statements like "I feel like I got fifty IQ points back!" "I'm plugged back in!" "I feel like I've woken up!"

BEHAVIOR

With the combination of lowered energy and limited motivation, the action in people's lives tends to decrease. There are many cancellations, lots of excuses. Often people concerned about their appearance become less interested in how they look. They find it difficult to initiate anything. All of these combine to create potential problems at work and home.

PHYSICAL CHANGES

Central to most depressive disorders are problems with sleep—either too much or too little. Similar differences are observed when it comes to appetite. Some people find themselves slowly losing their appetite with concurrent weight loss. For others, a noticeable increase in appetite is present. It is not unusual for depression to exist with other psychological and physical problems, such as eating and substance disorders, fibromyalgia, diabetes, cancer and heart disease.

THE GOOD NEWS

Depression can wreak havoc in every aspect of a sufferer's life. It also throws a wrench into the lives of those who care about the sufferer, rendering them helpless and frustrated. The good news? It is treatable. There is still no "magic bullet," but a wide variety of scientific advances make the picture for the depression sufferer far brighter now than ten or twenty years ago. Psychopharmacological (medicines) and psychotherapeutic (therapies) approaches are developing quickly. Alternative approaches are also being studied. Working with a mental-health professional, there is a high likelihood that many sufferers will find relief for the symptoms. It is important to note that dealing with depression is a collaboration, one that benefits from the inclusion of family members or friends as appropriate.

Talking to Depression represents the vast expanse beyond the one or two hours of professional mental-health contact most people get. In real life, friends, coworkers, family and other loved ones are the ones in the trenches with the depression sufferer. Claudia Strauss directs her words to those in the trenches, those who want to help but often aren't sure how. Those are the words that are often so rare, and yet so necessary. In a no-nonsense, practical approach, Strauss negotiates the land mines of depression as a knowing companion to her readers.

MARTHA MANNING

Preface

I wrote this book from my own experiences as well as from those of people I've known and worked with. We all have known someone who is depressed. Some of us are close to a person suffering from severe clinical depression. Some of us are concerned about other people in our lives who are struggling with depression. Over the years, I've learned that all of us have one important thing in common: We need to know we can make a difference. We need to know how to help. We need to know that everyday people in everyday situations can make a difference.

We tend to lose sight of that. We've come to feel that depression should be left to the professionals. With certification necessary as a license to practice in one field after another, we've become afraid to do what humans have done for other humans for thousands of years. We are afraid that we wouldn't know what to do because we haven't been trained, afraid we might make things worse, so we'd better do nothing.

This is a tragedy. The professionals aren't there in the moments of every day. They aren't there when we get up in the morning; they don't rush around with us as we try to get our day started; they're not with us in the workplace; they don't sit across from us at meals or next to us on the bus; they don't stroll with us at a mall or share a cup of coffee in the evening; they aren't there when we can't seem to get moving or feel we are going to dissolve.

And there is another thing to consider. Most of those professional consultations or sessions take place during the day. Depression doesn't shut off at night. If anything, without other distractions or other commitments, depression is most difficult to combat, most difficult to outlast, alone, raw during the hours of the night.

Professionals can't do it all and shouldn't be expected to. It's unrealistic. The professionals carve out a chunk of time one to four times a month and focus on us then. The rest of the time we're on our own. Professional help can make a tremendous difference to someone suffering from depression, but support from friends and family is a vital part of the recovery process. The person suffering from depression, family, friends, and professionals should all be partners in that process.

The people suffering from depression live their lives out in the world; they live their lives with us. The professions may be new, but the problems our friends and family members face are old. We can be there for them if we understand what they are facing. We can help them get through it; we can help them recover.

Knowing you can help is especially important when people do not seek professional help. And many people don't. They may not believe it can help them; they may not want their privacy invaded; they may feel there is something wrong about asking for help; they may not be able to afford it.

If you can find a way for them to accept help, great! If you can find a way for it to be paid for, wonderful! Depression is an illness like any other, and in many cases it can be successfully treated with therapy and/or medication. This book is not a substitute for either. It can only complement and supplement what professionals offer.

In the meantime, whether the people we care about are getting therapy or not, or medication or not, they will still benefit greatly from our presence, our caring, and our support.

I hope this book will give you the hope and confidence to help the people in your life that you are concerned about.

NOTE: I use "we" throughout this preface because we are all susceptible to depression. Some of us may get a mild case of it for a short time; for some of us it may be severe and long-lasting. For a sizeable proportion—one in ten of us every year—it will be diagnosed as clinical depression. However, in the rest of this book, both "you" and "we" will refer to those of us who are spending time with people we care about who are depressed. Whether "we" are depressed or not ourselves, we will be "we" in our role as loving friend and supportive family member of someone else who is depressed (short term) or suffering from depression (more long term).

Also, because depression can attack both male and female, in some paragraphs I use "he," "him," "his," and in others I refer to "she," "her," "hers." I tried to mix them up, and there is no particular reason for using one or the other in any particular paragraph.

Although I do provide some definitions and professional information, especially in the FAQ (Frequently Asked Questions) section that follows—which provides a brief overview of depression—I will not be focusing on clinical terms, approaches, medication, or recommendations of that sort. Nor will I focus on distinguishing one type of depression from another. However, where it would make a difference, I will point out when an approach tends to be more or less helpful. On the whole, this book will suggest things that are generally supportive of all sufferers of depression and that won't do them harm.

Part I

GETTING STARTED

"Look at reality with devotion."

🕊 MAY SARTON

Chapter One

An Overview of Depression

FREQUENTLY ASKED QUESTIONS

Some of you may have been struggling for a while on how to give support, but some of you may be entering unfamiliar territory. For those of you who are new to this, I thought it might be helpful to start by providing some general background information about depression. After this explanatory chapter, we'll move on to hands-on help—how to help the person you care about with words and actions as various situations arise.

WHAT IS DEPRESSION?

When we use this word in common speech, as laypeople, not doctors, we think of it as an extended period in which we feel particularly low, sad, uninterested, indecisive and unfocused. When doctors diagnose us as suffering from clinical depression, they are talking about an illness. They call it a mood disorder.

WHY DO THEY CALL IT A DISORDER?

Because depression is both qualitatively and quantitatively different from the blahs and the blues—in the same way flu is different from the sniffles, or pneumonia from the common cold. And because research has shown changes in body chemistry that may be associated with depression.

What's good about calling it a disease or disorder?

Three things. First, doctors are saying that depression is something they can treat. Second, they see it as something separate from the person—an invader such as an infection, a chemical imbalance such as diabetes, an ailment such as a limp. Depression is not "who" the person is; it's something the person "has." Third, and most important, they do not see it as anybody's fault—particularly not the fault of the person who is struggling with it.

Who gets depression?

Anyone can get it. In the United States, at any given time, 10 percent of adults are suffering from it—that's one in every ten adults. One in eight adolescents and one in thirty-three children get it, too. No background provides magic protection: not money or the lack of it, not religious background, ethnic background, racial background, educational level, career choice, or family makeup.

Is any group more likely to get depression?

Once puberty hits, gender seems to make a difference. Women are diagnosed with clinical depression far more often than men—in a ratio of 2:1. Part of that may be because of societal factors that are different for women. Part of that may be because of shifts in hormone levels. But part of that might also be because women are more likely to consult a professional and receive a diagnosis.

Regarding women in particular, depression can appear after childbirth and during menopause. It can also be developmental. Up to 5 percent of menstruating women suffer from depression associated with a severe form of PMS called Premenstrual Dysphoric Disorder (PMDD).

DO PEOPLE KNOW THEY ARE SUFFERING FROM DEPRESSION?

Not necessarily. More than half the people estimated to be suffering from depression have not sought help and many of them do not realize that what they are struggling with is depression. They may think they are stressed, scatterbrained, unfocused, burned out, impatient, or suffering from some physical ailment. Or they may think they are recovering from grief or trauma, unhappy in a relationship, or just not particularly happy or interested in their lives.

Those of us around them may think the same, or see anger or boredom and think it's directed at us and take it personally. We may interpret the symptoms as part of teenage rebellion and raging hormones, or see signs of depression and believe they are just typical of the slowing down, confusion and frustration of aging.

It can be hard to recognize depression. Throughout the book, we'll discuss ways you can learn to recognize it.

WHAT ARE THE SYMPTOMS OF DEPRESSION?

Mental-health professionals have established nine groups of symptoms. The rule of thumb for clinicians in diagnosing major (or clinical) depression is that someone has symptoms from five of these nine categories for a period of two weeks or longer. Professionals also look for symptoms that are intense enough to make it difficult for the patient to function at work, at home, or socially, and are enough of a change for other people to notice. Lastly, it means that other causes of these symptoms have been ruled out, such as another medical condition, side effects from a medication, substance abuse, or the natural effects of grieving in the first months after suffering a loss.

Below is a list of categories with examples of symptoms from each. This list is based on the DSM-IV framework of symptoms. The DSM-IV is the fourth edition of the *Diagnostic and Statistical Manual of Mental Disorders*, a standard resource of clinicians and insurance companies.

Nine Categories of Symptoms for
Major Depression

Changes in Mood—either appears to be in a depressed mood most of the time day after day, or says so. Could be moody, tearful, irritable, or talk about feeling sad or empty.

Lack of Pleasure—doesn't enjoy anything, doesn't feel anything, has no interest in anything, and this seems pretty consistent for most of the day and on most days.

Changes in Eating Patterns—either eating a lot more or eating a lot less day after day, or gaining or losing a significant amount of weight without being on a diet.

Changes in Sleeping Patterns—either having trouble sleeping day after day or sleeping much more than usual day after day.

Changes in Activity Level and Movement—either very slow at reacting to what people say and at getting moving or following through in any physical activity—including walking, talking, coordination, etc., or agitated, restless, and unable to stop moving in some way. And this can be seen by other people, not just felt, and it seems to be present for most of the day and on most days.

Lack of Energy—excessive tiredness, fatigue, and lack of energy to do things one normally could do, day after day.

Changes in Perception of Self—a new and persistent sense of guilt, of worthlessness, of inadequacy, nearly every day, about oneself in general, not about the depression itself.

Changes in Focus—such as lack of concentration, forgetfulness, inability to think, inability to make decisions, occurring nearly every day.

Lack of Future—thoughts of hopelessness, death, suicide (either with a plan or without one), or an attempt at suicide.

Remember that there are no absolutes about this; these are just guidelines. It's important to keep this in mind because there is considerable overlapping as well as individual combinations of symptoms. Let a professional decide these things.

How do I tell the difference between grief and depression?

Grief is a reaction to loss—or to something that has happened that is very painful. If a number of months pass and a person who has been grief-stricken seems to sink deeper into grief, if he isolates himself more than he had before, if she seems less able to manage everyday chores and work functions than in the earlier months, and if you see other symptoms of depression appearing, then there might be cause for concern.

It's important to remember, though, that while grief can be intense, most people don't develop depression as a result of it. Working through grief is a process that can take several months to a couple of years. But it is a process that tends to move forward.

Grief is normal, and most people go through a series of steps in more or less the same order before reaching a level of recovery. Some people, though, may cycle through some of the steps several times before moving forward.

It's also important to remember that the first days or weeks of grief can seem muted because the person is in shock and protecting himself from the grief. While he is coping with the shock and dealing with the demands of the situation, he is not yet fully absorbing the grief. So "counting" that a number of months has passed shouldn't start until after the first shock has lifted and the person you care about is letting herself feel the pain.

If I suspect depression, what I should do?

A good first step is to suggest the person visit a doctor. Many of the symptoms of depression are physical and the cause can be physical too. A doctor will do a work-up to consider all the possibilities. She might have a vitamin deficiency. He might have sleep apnea. Maybe something is interfering with the flow of oxygen to the brain. Maybe it's a reaction to medications she is taking. Maybe his thyroid isn't functioning properly. Maybe she is going through hormonal changes. It could be any number of things, most of which are treatable.

The important thing is to determine if the symptoms that look like depression are really symptoms of another medical condition. If he goes to a medical doctor first, that would be where the physician starts. If she goes to a mental-health professional first, possible medical causes would be explored, too. And a mental-health professional will often refer her to a medical doctor to rule out the most common suspects.

WHAT IF ALL THESE ARE ELIMINATED AND THE DOCTOR THINKS IT'S DEPRESSION? WHAT THEN?

That depends on three things: who they see next, what kind of depression they have, and how they would like to proceed.

One person might continue with the family doctor. Another might see a specialist, such as a mental-health professional. Then it depends on the specialist. Some can prescribe medications; some can't. Some focus on one kind of therapy, some on another. Some people decide to see two kinds of specialists—a person who will address body chemistry and a person who will provide a form of counseling therapy; in that case it's a good idea to pick professionals who have a working relationship with each other so they can coordinate what they do. In fact, it's best if everyone, including the person struggling with depression, works together as partners.

There are a number of different kinds of specialists. These include medical specialists, such as psychiatrists, neurologists, and gerontologists; counseling specialists, such as psychologists, social workers, and counselors; complementary and alternative medicine specialists, such as nutritionists, chiropractors, acupuncturists, herbalists, massage therapists, and other holistic healers. In addition, a number of techniques, such as biofeedback, aromatherapy, relaxation techniques, meditation, and light therapy can be added to a treatment plan. People suffering from depression will work with their doctor or primary therapist to choose which of these options to pursue.

Some people choose to do nothing. They may feel a need to tackle this on their own. Unless they are a danger to themselves or others, that is their choice.

Often people take time to consider what they want to do next, what kind of treatment they want to consider, and what kind of provider they want to work with. Sometimes they need to come to terms with what they have before they can reach out for help.

WHAT GETS IN THE WAY OF PEOPLE SEEKING TREATMENT?

Pride. Shame. Privacy. Money. Myths.

Many people think their symptoms come from laziness, lack of discipline, a character flaw, unworthiness, or punishment from God. Or that people will never view them in the same way if they admit to suffering from a mental illness and get help. Or that having a mental illness means they somehow brought it on themselves. Or that if they brought it on themselves, they should be able to turn it around themselves, too, and if they can't, they are less than other people.

This is sad, because there are all kinds of treatment approaches and most people can be helped when the right treatment match is found. And this is sad, too, because the person and the depression are two separate entities. The depression will not define who the person is. It will change his mood, affect his life, affect his ability to act the way he normally would, but it will not become him. He did not choose to be stricken with depression any more than he would choose any other serious illness, nor can he just tell it to go away, any more than he could tell his heart, pancreas or liver to resume functioning properly.

You can encourage treatment by letting him know about where to get confidential screenings, or even anonymous ones on the Web. Maybe a mutual relative or friend could help you encourage him to explore treatment options. Let him know that not getting treatment could make it harder to overcome the depression and may result in other illnesses: depression can affect the immune system; it puts people at risk for heart disease; and people suffering from depression are more likely to die after heart surgery. Let him see that shortening a bout of depression, or lessening its impact, makes sense, and that looking for answers and consulting an expert means he is taking charge of the situation.

ARE TREATMENTS SUCCESSFUL?

Most people who seek treatment find relief. But about half of those who struggle with depression once go on to have another episode. And a large proportion of those end up with recurrent episodes. It is believed that in these people, the body may have found (or formed) neural pathways to do this and keeps "re-creating" the depression. It's like riding a bicycle—once we've learned how to do it, it comes automatically and we never forget it. Except that, unlike bike riding, depression is something we don't want to repeat.

For these people, who struggle repeatedly, medication can help. With medication, episodes are fewer, further apart, and less severe. Often, dosages have to be adjusted and they may need to shift from one medication to another. Sometimes, a cliché turns out to be the best guide: "The dosage that makes you well will keep you well." For many people, cutting back the dosage after a recurrent episode of depression lifts can put them at risk. So any adjustments to medication need to be done under careful monitoring by a doctor.

Some medication dosages can be monitored through blood tests. And, as with all multiple medication situations, any interactions should be monitored, too. Those suffering from depression can take a frontline role by tracking their symptoms, medications, dosages and any changes in what they feel, say, or do. Documenting this kind of information on a regular basis in a journal facilitates adjustments happening sooner rather than later. However, not everyone will be able to do this, and the depression itself may interfere with a person's ability to be organized and follow through.

WHAT KIND OF MEDICATION IS AVAILABLE FOR DEPRESSION?

There are numerous medications available, and new breakthroughs are being made every day. Most medications shift the body's chemical balance, impeding or promoting the body's production of certain chemicals and their ability to act.

When medication is used, it is important to remember that everyone will respond differently. For example, someone who is having trouble sleeping will do better with certain antidepressants, while someone who is constantly sleeping will do better with others. Someone who is very anxious may do better with medications that have a sedative effect, while others may do better with a stimulant.

If medication is necessary, it's a good idea to work with a doctor who is familiar with a wide range of medications, like a psychiatrist. A general practitioner might not have the depth of experience in this specialized area to tailor the treatment to the person you care about.

The practice of medicine is part science and part art, and the doctor and patient have to be partners in the treatment process. This is particularly true for depression, where both the drug and the dosages may need adjustments and fine-tuning, and where antidepressants might have to be combined with other medications to stabilize mood or treat anxiety.

WHAT KIND OF THERAPY SHOULD HE CHOOSE?

The two kinds of therapy that have been most effective in controlling depression are cognitive/behavioral and interpersonal therapy. There are many approaches to cognitive/behavioral, but they all work to change ways of thinking and ways of acting, not just in general, but when one feels symptoms of depression coming on. The idea is to create alternate neural pathways. One way to understand this is to consider what the constant practice of an athlete or musician is designed to do—to make certain movements smooth and automatic. It's always easier for them to reach this point if they learn good habits and procedures from the outset.

In terms of depression, a person may not have bad habits, but he may have ineffective ones that lead to depression. What cognitive/behavioral therapy tries to do is find a path that works and help the patient to stay on it. The idea is to help the patient avoid getting on the wrong mental path, because that would trigger a chemical reaction that would bring about depression.

Interpersonal therapy focuses on the person's relationship with his spouse, children, parents or coworkers because sometimes something in a relationship can act as an environmental trigger. The goal is to improve these relationships by helping a person set boundaries, confront and reframe troublesome issues, and renegotiate how the relationship will work. It also helps a person recognize the support provided by the positive personal connections already in place, and figure out how to find sustenance in them. Positive connection in itself can help to create change.

ARE THERE OTHER APPROACHES TO TREATMENT?

Yes. While medications and therapy each work well on their own, they often work best when combined. And combining these with other approaches helps, too. Treating other factors contributing to the depression can both speed up the recovery process and help the person who is suffering take control of the depression.

Adding antianxiety medications and mood stabilizers is becoming commonplace. But doctors are trying additional ways to multiply the effects of antidepressants, such as balancing out hormone levels (especially estrogen or testosterone), supplementing the production of essential chemicals that regulate body function (such as thyroid hormones), and finding ways to control the hormones involved with stress.

There is also an approach used long ago that has become very effective and much safer, and that is electroconvulsive therapy (ECT), a form of shock therapy in which electric current is applied to the surface of the skull. This is a successful way to get people out of a severe depression. Once controversial, technological advances have made it something professionals will recommend when other treatments haven't worked. It is not what you have seen in old movies; people are sedated so the procedure is painless and are given a muscle relaxant so that, though muscles tense up, convulsive shaking no longer occurs. Doctors also have a lot more control over how they administer the current.

As with medications, there can be side effects. In the case of ECT, a small number (about 5 percent) experience memory loss that may be serious. Sometimes the memory loss is temporary. Sometimes it is extensive, sometimes not. Because of this, ECT tends to be a treatment of last resort, and doctor and patient should have a complete discussion of the risks and benefits before proceeding.

The same sort of discussion should take place before using alternative or complementary approaches, because nothing works in isolation. Herbals and botanicals, for example, will interact with other medications, whether they are antidepressive or targeted at something else. They can stop other medications from working, or they can multiply their effects. Either can put a person at risk, so it's important to involve doctor and pharmacist in all forms of treatment and keep them informed about other therapies. This is true even if they are not medications or food derivatives that are ingested (such as acupuncture). Monitoring the results will help the doctor-patient-family team figure out what is working.

ARE THERE DIFFERENT KINDS OF DEPRESSION?

Yes. And there are a number of ways to look at them.

By frequency (one-time, episodic/recurrent, chronic):

Some people experience a major bout of depression one time in their lives. A smaller group gets episodes at various times; it tends to hit them over and over again. And for others it's chronic; it's always there at some level, though its intensity, severity, effect on mood and effect on ability to function will fluctuate.

By symptoms (uni- vs. bipolar):

Most people suffer from unipolar depression (also called "major depression"), which means they feel an extreme version of feeling "down" or they lose the ability to feel at all. They can't get themselves going, have trouble functioning, withdraw from people.

Some people (20 percent of those who struggle with depression) suffer from bipolar disorder, also known as manic-depression. People who suffer from it swing from one extreme to another, from a weighed-down depressive state to a manic state in which they have too much energy, can't channel all of it, and try to do twenty-seven things before lunch. In manic states, they can feel elated, anxious, irritable, and overflowing with thoughts and the desire to put them into action. This can be terribly disruptive and include delusions, leading to horrible decisions and dangerous actions. Someone in a manic phase can feel as much out of control as he does in the depressive phase, losing the ability to focus, feel grounded, or feel connected.

They may welcome help in the depressive phase but resist treatment in the manic phase. Some may use alcohol or street drugs to control the mania, but many look forward to this upswing phase. It makes them feel pumped, productive, creative, super-energized. They don't want medications because they fear the homogenizing of their emotions, the flattening of their mood. They are willing to live through the horrible lows to get the creative highs. They are afraid they won't be the same people if they "lose" the disease.

By severity (mild, moderate, severe):

It helps to have a sense of different levels of severity, but even clinicians struggle with deciding where someone fits overall, and people can shift from up or down, in or out, of these areas. But typically, severe depression is diagnosed when a person's ability to get through daily life is drastically reduced. The inability to get out of bed, crying all the time, and being unable to focus on conversation are all associated with severe depression. Moderate symptoms tend to be frequent, intense, and to interfere with work and personal relationships, and often include lack of energy, constant fatigue, and changes in appetite and sleep patterns. Mild depression is often associated with a feeling of numbness, trouble concentrating, forgetfulness, and an inability to feel pleasure.

By cause (external or internal; genetic or situational; chemistry-dictated or chemistry-reactive):

Depression can be a reaction to an outside event—grief, trauma, betrayal, loss of a job, or some other external event. It can come from major physical trauma, such as surgery, a heart attack, or an accident. It can develop from ongoing, persistent stress. It can come from childbirth (postpartum depression) and from lack of sunlight (seasonal affective disorder). It can also come from diseases that affect mental functioning, such as Alzheimer's or stroke. It can also come about from internal struggles over issues such as identity, self-worth, making sense of the world, or loss of a relationship.

Some people are predisposed to depression because of their genetic makeup. Depression, especially bipolar disorder, appears to run in their families, not because the depressed person has learned it or witnessed it, but because it's in their genes. The strength of the predisposition seems to vary from person to person, and a person's temperament can be a factor, too.

Some people suffering from depression have been found to have different levels of chemicals involved in brain function. It is not known which comes first, the depression or the chemical changes. Some think that certain people have a genetic predisposition to a chemical imbalance, but that it has to be triggered by something in the environment. Others think that the depression comes first, and that the depression itself changes the chemical balance, that no genetic marker is involved or needs to be. What is known is that these kinds of chemical changes also occur among people suffering from stress and trauma.

ARE THERE OTHER SITUATIONS IN WHICH DEPRESSION EXISTS?

Yes. Depression is associated with a number of disorders, most commonly with anxiety disorders. Some examples include: attention deficit disorder (ADD), attention deficit hyperactivity disorder (ADHD), learning disabilities, conduct disorder, obsessive compulsive disorder (OCD), and eating disorders. Any one of these can exist together with depression and often does. For example, a person can have ADD, a learning disability, and depression. If one of these is diagnosed, it's worth checking to see if depression is present. And the reverse is true—just as one of these may be masking depression,

depression can be masking another disorder. For example, attention problems are often a symptom of depression, yet they are also a hallmark of ADD. It's important to know which one a person is dealing with, or whether both are present. Each has an effect on the quality of a person's life, and that quality can only be improved if both of them are addressed.

DOES THE TYPE OF DEPRESSION DICTATE THE FORM OF TREATMENT?

Yes and no. Yes, because it will determine a starting place. Diagnosing the type of depression will guide a doctor in what to prescribe— medications, therapy, or a combination—and in what order. For example, someone with mild depression might start with therapy alone and possibly add medications later.

HOW QUICKLY DOES TREATMENT WORK?

Medications tend to work more quickly than other forms of treatment, often providing some relief within two to four weeks. One symptom in particular—sleep problems—will respond quickly. This can make a person feel such a difference that he thinks he can stop the medication, but a person needs to continue the medication for at least three months to significantly lift the depression.

Many cases of major depression—especially first ones—lift within six months regardless of the type of treatment or whether there is any treatment at all, though some depression lasts for years. Treatment is worthwhile, though, because it lifts the depression faster and can help prevent a less severe form from sliding into a more severe form. It can also soften and reduce the symptoms. This can protect a person's quality of life by preserving relationships, jobs, and financial stability. This decreases pain and suffering for families, friends, and coworkers, too.

WHEN DOESN'T TREATMENT WORK?

Sometimes it's a matter of finding the right match—the medication, counseling approach, or therapist that just fits. We have all experienced this in other situations. Maybe the first medication doesn't take care of the ear infection, so the doctor prescribes something else. Maybe we shop around for the gynecologist who makes us most comfortable, or try several dentists before we settle on one. In treating depression, "fit" is extremely important. Mental health professionals understand that, and understand that people may need to shop around.

If the person struggling with depression doesn't see progress over a period of time, he should discuss his concern with the professional he is seeing. If he is taking a medication (or combining medications), there may be guidelines on how long it usually takes before he is likely to feel a difference. She should understand the reasoning behind the treatment plan. He should ask about other options. Change and flexibility are a vital part of treatment.

Sometimes, as can happen with other diseases, the depression is resistant to any form of treatment. Support becomes even more crucial as the person suffering from it has to find a way to live with it and wait for some relief.

WHY MIGHT DEPRESSION CAUSE THE PERSON TO ENGAGE IN UNHEALTHY BEHAVIOR?

Many people suffering from depression look for ways to cope, but the paths they choose are not always constructive. People in the manic phases of bipolar disorder may use drinking, street drugs, and over-the-counter medications to control their mania, to find a way to slow down when they can't stop on their own. People suffering from unipolar depression, on the other hand, will use these to either deaden pain or to feel some sort of exhilaration. The layperson may think that this behavior is causing the depression; instead, it is the other way around. The depression is causing these forms of self-medication. If you are seeing this behavior, it could be a symptom of an underlying depression.

Substance abuse is not the only unproductive way in which people try to cope. If they are in pain, they isolate themselves so they can't feel— not just externally, by avoiding people, but internally, by avoiding any emotion. This means they wall themselves off from pleasure, too. Some, who can't focus and have lost belief in themselves, at first choose not to make decisions or act at all. Then they lose the capacity to do so, and can appear paralyzed. Others, to avoid thinking, feeling, or facing any of these problems, become frenetic. They are always in motion, always working, always filling their minds with thoughts and their hands with activities. Sometimes this is their way of controlling their emotions, but they may get stuck and lose the ability to slow down even if they want to.

CAN I GET INVOLVED IN TREATMENT?

There are all kinds of ways to provide support that are discussed in the following pages. They focus on what you as a layperson can do. However, there may be situations where you want to get involved in treatment, or when the person you care about may ask you to talk to her doctor or his therapist. This will not always be automatic, because there are laws regarding confidentiality. If you are the parent of a minor child, the guardian of an adult or a child, or have power of attorney, the professional will talk to you. Otherwise, the adult you care about will have to sign a release to permit the professional to include you in discussions.

"Although the world is very full of suffering, it is also full of the overcoming of it."

— HELEN KELLER

Chapter Two

Where to Start

DECIDING YOU CAN HELP

WADING IN

Depression is overwhelming. When someone we know is struggling with it, we may want to help, but we also want to run away. That's natural. Depression is scary. We see someone we care about being sucked down and we don't know how to help. We don't even know if help is possible.

We wonder so many things. What if I say the wrong thing? What if I make it worse? What if I push too hard? What if I don't push hard enough? What if I'm not there at the crucial moment? What if I let her become dependent on me? What if he never gets better?

We worry about ourselves. What if I get upset all the time? What if she keeps calling in the middle of the night? What if he calls me at work? What if I can't make a difference and she keeps sinking? How do I keep from sinking with him?

We question when to intervene. How can I tell that he is a danger to himself? If I do intervene, will he trust me anymore?

Perhaps we have experienced this before and we can remember failing in our efforts, being pushed away, being yelled at, and gradually feeling lower and lower ourselves as we seemed to gain no ground yet steadily felt our own energy seeping away.

There are no perfect answers. The key is to follow your gut. Listen with your mind and with your heart, with your body and your skin. Think about how you feel when you're down. What kind of response helps you? What kind of response generates negative feelings?

The hardest thing to do is not to judge, but if you can manage that, you won't push the person away. Because the most important thing for a person who is depressed is to continue to feel connected, continue to feel respected and continue to feel worthwhile.

DETERMINING YOUR ROLE

Ideally, when you decide to help someone with depression, you will be part of a network of friends and family, each providing their own form of support. And, ideally, some of you will know one another, so you can support each other, too. But sometimes you are the only person who is in a position to reach the depressed person. Sometimes there are others, but you are the closest to the depressed person.

Wherever you stand in the constellation of friends and family surrounding the depressed person, only you can determine your role. This may seem scary, but remember how you define your role now doesn't have to be perfect or permanent. Your role can keep on changing as circumstances change, as the depression changes, and as your relationship changes. This is an ongoing process—you will always be determining it.

What does your role depend on? What you can give. What the person you care about is prepared to accept. It depends on how close you are and whether you are accustomed to depending on one another. It depends on the type of people you both are. Open, confiding people will be able to accept help. Other more private people might need to be in control. Both of you will struggle with the issue of control. You, because you can't just charge in and fix everything, and he because accepting help means acknowledging he has lost control.

Your role can also depend on legal relationships. Are you married to each other? Are you the parent of a minor child? Has the person you care about told you what's wrong? Has she shared a diagnosis or asked you to participate in therapy?

And in addition to all these things, your role depends on the severity of the depression, at what point in the process you become involved, and whether you know other people who have a closer relationship than you do with the person you care about—perhaps someone you can alert to what you see so you can enlist support.

You need to consider all these things when you want to define your role, but there is always something you can say or do to help him make steps toward recovery.

You are not the cure, but you can provide the environment and the staying power and the confidence that will nurture recovery. Without the proper soil, necessary nutrients, and the warmth of the sun, plants can't grow. Lifting oneself out of depression requires these things, too. In facing a great battle, we all need to know there's someone behind us who believes in us and our capacity to fight. Battling depression requires time—sometimes a lot of time. It's a long dark tunnel and one can't travel around it—one can only travel through it.

The key to providing support is sustaining your own frame of mind. The most important thing is to continue to really *see* this person you care about—who she is at her core—and to feel the respect you have always felt for her, the joy you have felt in her presence. Don't let the disease become who he is.

You have all the tools to do this: knowledge, memories, love, imagination. Remind yourself of them and continue to treat the person as you always have—with respect, humor, camaraderie. When we continue to see the person as whole, he will feel it, and much of what it is best to do and say will come naturally.

WHAT IF I'M FAR AWAY?

Sometimes being far away is a plus. It is often easier to provide support when you're not immersed in the situation every day. When you don't live in the same house or work together, it's more likely that there will be balance in your life, opportunities to refresh yourself. And distance doesn't have to affect frequency. Modern technology has made sure of that. You can call, e-mail and write her. Your voices can mingle; your words can reach her. Every time you touch her mind you can touch her heart. Art Buchwald called Mike Wallace every day during the months Wallace was struggling with depression. Every day. It made a difference, and Mike Wallace has not stopped talking about it.

The person on the scene every day must find ways to sustain himself while finding time to focus on the person struggling with depression. He must learn to change the knee-jerk communication responses that come from thousands and millions of previous interactions with that person and learn a new way of relating. He must also cope with his own sense of powerlessness and feelings of being overwhelmed.

BURNING OUT

Planning for yourself is important, too. How much of yourself will you be able to give in terms of time, emotion, and energy? Telling someone you'll be there for her may be one of the best things you can say, but saying you'll be there is a commitment.

It takes serious consideration. But getting in without burning out and getting out without doing damage are both possible. It depends on how you handle the situation from the beginning. And, like most everything else in life, there is no black and white here. Things are relative.

Maybe she needs you now, but later she'll need someone else more. Maybe you can listen and provide the warmth that he needs now, but when he's ready for structure and a push, there'll be someone else who can fill that role. This doesn't mean you disappear entirely, but eventually you may take a backseat. You wait and see when it is appropriate to reduce either the length or the frequency of your contacts. What's important is that you don't change the quality of your interactions.

You can set boundaries, such as, "When you really need to talk, call me—anytime, even in the middle of the night. Just not every night. Okay?" Or, "How about if we talk at three p.m. tomorrow, and get together for coffee on Friday at five fifteen?" Or, "I expect to be in a work crunch next week, so would it be okay if we touch base late at night, say around ten p.m.?"

There is nothing wrong with leaving messages for them to find: notes, cards, voice mail, or e-mail letting them know you are thinking of them.

YOU CAN SAY:

- "Really busy lately, but thinking of you."
- "Just wanted to let you know I'm thinking of you."
- "Drop me a line and let me know what's happening with you."

- "Looking forward to bringing you up-to-date on what's been going on."
- "I don't know where the week went! Think we could grab some coffee next week? When's good for you?"

Setting limits like this will help you stand by your commitment to help through the long haul. Don't feel like you are copping out by setting limits. Do it in a clear and supportive way. And remember, limits will help you be there when the person you care about needs you most.

"Pain doesn't come with an expiration date."

➤ CLAUDIA J. STRAUSS

Chapter Three

Seeing Through Their Eyes

What Depression Feels Like

If you haven't suffered from depression yourself, it helps to understand what the person you care about is going through. Knowing something about what it actually feels like will help you provide more effective support. What does depression feel like? You can see someone's sadness, or sense how disconnected she is. You might notice his indecision, loss of appetite, or sloppy appearance. You might notice she keeps missing work or can't get work done. But these are all things you are observing from the outside. What does it feel like from the inside?

In this chapter you will hear the voices of people who have suffered from depression or are suffering now. I've gathered these comments from what people have said to me over the years and from what I have said to them. There are five sections: First, what depression feels like when it has one in its grip. Second, where it comes from. Third, what helps the most when one is going through it. Fourth, what gets in the way. Fifth, how meaningful it is to have family and friends who care.

Even when suffering from depression, there is a part of the sufferer that is observing, that recognizes that friends and family members are trying to help and realizes how difficult his unresponsiveness is for the people who care about him. In the fifth section of this chapter, those who have struggled acknowledge this. It will help you to hear them express gratitude, explain what the effort means to them, provide absolution for those who tried to help.

Everyone has different temperaments, different thresholds for pain, and different abilities to manage it. Everyone has different coping mechanisms, different inner resources and outside support systems. Some people are active in nature, some passive. Some are gregarious, some isolated. Some are dramatic, some reserved. Some overstate things, some understate.

Everyone perceives things differently and uses language differently, which is why behavior is often more reliable than words in determining how deep his depression is, what kind of depression she has, or how likely he is to hurt himself. The words he selects to describe his feelings might not be the words we would select, so we might not interpret them correctly. That is why the symptoms listed in the first chapter are things we can observe.

Still, it is important to understand what this suffering feels like. By listening to different voices, you will be able to get a fuller, rounder, clearer picture of what it is like to live with depression. It will become real.

WHAT DOES DEPRESSION FEEL LIKE?

- "A feeling of despair, grief."
- "A lack of hope."
- "A feeling of incompetence, incapacity."
- "A feeling of an unyielding, unrepairable life."
- "If someone touched me, I'd shatter like glass—I crave to be touched but I can't risk it."

- "If someone touched me, I'd cling. I wouldn't be able to let go."
- "Everyone avoids me. I'm not contagious. They throw walls around themselves and keep themselves as separate as they can. They are afraid of my pain—afraid it will be their pain. I know that, but it feels as if they don't care, they can't be bothered, that no one can help, that I'm all alone and on my own with this, that it must not be solvable, that I'm not worthy."
- "It's like I'm closed in—this wall separating me from everyone else, from feeling things."
- "Always on edge, always about to implode or explode."
- "Time seems like a huge hole that sucks one in . . . and it needs to be filled so one can be distracted from it."
- "I can't remember who I am, what I'm good at, why anyone would like me, or what I used to enjoy doing—it's all gone, or buried somewhere. I can't find it, I don't know where to look, and I don't have the energy to look—what's the point?"
- "I feel paralyzed. Can't do anything. Can't think of anything. Only aware of pain and/or emptiness."
- "Raw, without a skin, feeling a lot and feeling empty, all at the same time."
- "Feeling cold and hot at the same time."
- "Overwhelmed with nothingness, no hope."
- "Unable to bear the thought of any more pain, for any longer."
- "Totally without energy, unable to decide anything, unable to move, or think, or see or hear."
- "As if I'm not intact. There are pieces missing. Irreplaceable."
- "Empty. A zombie. Staring at walls, but not seeing anything, not thinking anything. Blank."
- "Angry. Reliving nightmares over and over. But they are real.

They play in my mind all day. No matter what I'm doing. I can't shut them out."
- "Dead. I've already died. There's nothing there. This can't be my body that walks around and talks. Because I'm not in it. I don't exist anymore. Why don't others see that? They don't want to see."
- "Sometimes I feel as if I've been erased. I'm invisible; I don't exist."
- "It lives inside me. It pretends to be me."

WHERE DOES IT SEEM TO COME FROM?

- "I wish I knew."
- "It just came out of nowhere."
- "It's in my family. A chemical imbalance. Imagine, being born depressed."
- "No one knows why. It just is."
- "It started with grief. It turned into this. I don't know when."
- "Things happened. It felt like rape. Nothing made sense afterwards."
- "My doctor thinks I lost purpose when I retired. She wishes I'd had a hobby or something planned. It was never about anything except work. I'm really lost when I get up in the morning."
- "It's not the first time. I seem to be more vulnerable to this now."
- "Maybe it was too many things at once. Tough things. Sad things. Scary things. Major responsibilities. It makes burning out feel manageable."

- "Guilt. It just gnaws at me and gnaws at me until I'm not sure there *is* a me."
- "Failure."
- "String of bad luck."
- "Abuse."
- "Stress."
- "Faulty wiring."

WHAT KIND OF SUPPORT HELPS THE MOST?

- "Knowing I can call day or night."
- "Helping me with structure."
- "Just listening and listening and listening."
- "Not pretending to understand or telling their own story over and over."
- "If they've been there, how it felt, and what helped—being specific and graphic about it."
- "Checking up on me."
- "Not getting angry."
- "Not judging."
- "Creating times to be together."
- "Understanding that sometimes I just need to be around someone, but that talking would be too much work."
- "Understanding that sometimes I can't stand to be around anyone."
- "Not letting me feel embarrassed or guilty for being stuck in this place."
- "Pointing out that it takes a lot of time—you can't get un-stuck overnight."

- "Understanding that it takes a lot of work and energy, more energy than anything else, even though it's not visible."
- "Understanding that hope is cruel—I can't afford to hope anymore."
- "Giving me another picture of hope. If hope is seen as something one travels toward, then it's not a matter of it not coming to you, it's a matter of your not having arrived there yet. This way, hope is an objective, not an ever-present thing that keeps getting broken or snatched away."
- "Asking me how I do it. How I am managing to get through the days. How I keep going. How I deal with it. And asking me this with awe in their voices."
- "Telling me how proud they are of me and why."
- "Reminding me of all the good things I have done in my life."
- "Reminding me of what a good friend I've been."
- "Reminding me of all the things I know, all the things I can do, that I'm capable."
- "Loving me, and saying so."
- "Asking me if there's a way I want to be pushed or pulled into doing something. Asking me to let you know when I'm ready for that and then following through."
- "Doing things with me that produce creative or practical results that I can see."
- "Helping me dream again. Helping me see the possibility of a future."
- "Helping me reconnect; doing it with me to get me started."

WHAT HURTS? GETS IN THE WAY? SETS ME BACK?

- "People insisting I do something I'm not ready to do."
- "People getting angry when I can't or won't follow their advice."
- "Constantly talking to me about depression or asking questions about it regardless of whether I want to discuss it or not. Sometimes it helps to talk about something else."
- "Treating me like a stubborn child."
- "Believing I'm just lazy."
- "Telling me to snap out of it."
- "Telling me this has gone on long enough, as if grief has a timetable."
- "Telling me if I decide to be happy, I will be."
- "Not respecting my request to change the subject, to back off."
- "Acting as if I'm an embarrassment."
- "Telling me they are ashamed of my behavior."
- "Talking about me in front of other people."
- "Not respecting my privacy."
- "Disappearing from my life."
- "Not calling when they said they would. Sometimes the only way I get through the days is by knowing that call will be there at the end of them."

WHAT WOULD YOU SAY TO FAMILY AND FRIENDS WHO TRY TO HELP?

- "I may not make it through all this, but you haven't failed."
- "Your being here is the only light I have."
- "With depression, there is no quality of life. It's a separate world. You are a messenger from another world, *the* other world. You bring it to me and help me breathe some of its air. Without that, I couldn't fight the battles I do fight. I couldn't win the battles I have won."
- "You didn't bring on this war. If I've made any progress in getting out, it's due to you. You have created miracles when I thought they were impossible."
- "I know I've been really difficult, uncooperative, resistant to everything you suggest. It just takes more energy than I can summon up. That's not your failure; that just comes with the territory."
- "You chose to stay. No matter how I acted. No matter how I treated you. No matter how often I relapsed. Whether I was high or low. Even when it sucked the life out of you. Even though I can't tell you or show you that it matters. You chose to stay. It matters."
- "You are the closest to an angel that I could imagine."
- "You prolonged my life and gave it glimpses of meaning. No one else was able to do that."
- "I hope you will never need this, but if you should ever face what I have faced, I hope there will be someone to do for you all that you have done for me."
- "That you tried means everything."

Part II

What to Say

"*There is a commonplace idea, accepted by nearly everyone, that feelings become blunted by experience. Nothing could be more untrue.*"

✹ Victor Hugo

Chapter Four

Opening the Conversation

First Things to Say

Whether you are a friend or relative, a neighbor or coworker, once you have decided to help someone with depression, the first question you will have is, How? Not being a professional doesn't mean you don't have something important to give. What you give is yourself, the immediacy of caring. Just being there is a crucial kind of support. But once you're there, what do you do?

The answer to this question is the core of this book. Because the biggest question anyone in your position has is, What do I say? Some words can help, others can hurt. Some words can reach the person you care about, and some can't. The next few chapters will help you choose the words that help.

This chapter focuses on your first conversation. On how to bring up the subject of depression in a gradual, respectful, and sensitive way.

Opening a conversation with someone who has been depressed for a long time or who has recently suffered a terrible loss can be daunting. It can feel awkward or insensitive to ask "How are you?" or "How's it going?" It may be painful for the person to say "fine," or she may feel she's telling a lie.

If you follow it up with "How are you, really?" she may feel put on the spot. Or she may resent your bringing it up because she's barely holding on and just being asked about it will set off tears; on the other hand, she may be grateful that you are not avoiding her pain.

How are you to know how she feels about it? How are you to know if this is a time for distractions or a time for revelations? A time for venting and hand-holding or a time for putting it aside for a while and moving forward in some way?

START WITH A QUESTION.

Sometimes just talking is difficult, no matter what the subject, and it may be a while before they can talk about their situation. This becomes increasingly true as depression moves from mild to moderate to severe. Language, like everything else, becomes more difficult to process. In such cases, you should know that just getting a general conversation started helps, and it's better to not ask too many questions at once. Leave a lot of room for pauses when you talk, and try not to fill all the silences yourself. Be patient.

- "Do you want to talk?"
- "Do you feel like talking? We could talk about it or we could talk about other things. Whatever you want."
- "Do you want to talk about it? I'd be happy to listen as long as you like, and then we could talk about other stuff or go do something. Or we could just go do stuff, if you like. What would you prefer?"

ASK IN THE FORM OF A STATEMENT.

Sometimes people have a need to talk about things but have difficulty bringing them up or are afraid to impose. You can give them the opportunity by opening the door. And by giving them choices, you also make it possible for them to say "no" graciously. Just be sure to respect their refusal, be it gracious or otherwise.

- "I don't know what you want to do today. I'm open to whatever you want to do."
- "We could talk or not talk. Talk about how you're feeling or talk about something else."
- "We could vent or figure things out, or just do something distracting."
- "We could go somewhere, or we could sit here together. That's always nice."

LET THEM TAKE THE LEAD.

- "I don't know whether you want me to push you into doing something today or not. You tell me."

BE UPBEAT.

- "Hey, you told me to push. I took my orders from you, remember?"
- "Come on. We're going to try this."
- "Let's go!"
- "Hold on, here we go."

TREAT THEM WITH RESPECT.

They're adults. Treat them with respect and they will reciprocate. If they gave the go-ahead to push, they may pull back a little but they will try to follow through. It was their decision, and they'll recognize that. On the other hand, they may change their minds. That's okay. You can always try another time.

But don't push too hard or prod and poke at their minds. They're still there. Being lost should not affect your respect for them or how you treat them. Dignity and feeling like peers matter a lot.

"It takes an enormous amount of energy just to be normal."

✎ ALBERT CAMUS

Chapter Five

Words That Wound

What Not to Say

*I*n the world of depression, sometimes the most well-meant phrases can do the most damage. It is as important to think about what *not* to say as it is to choose words of comfort.

This chapter gives examples of common expressions that don't work well with people who are suffering from depression. Becoming aware of these and understanding why they backfire will help you avoid them.

These examples bear a resemblance to one another in the way they affect the person who hears them. Once you see how they are similar, you will be able to avoid saying other versions of them.

"It's not that bad."

This is one of the worst things to say to someone suffering from depression. You may be trying to give perspective with the reminder that all things pass, but that is not what the person hears. What the person *hears* is that you don't take him seriously, that his pain is small compared to what it could be. What the person *feels* is that you are challenging his perceptions and his judgment. What the person *fears* is that you are accusing him of being weak, of being unable to face a challenge.

You might say, "It's not that bad" because you want him to find a way to move forward. You expect he'll feel some relief that you think this challenge can be overcome. You expect him to pull himself together with your help.

Instead, your statement puts him in a corner. Now he needs to defend his feelings and to justify his perceptions. And the more he explains and defends and justifies them, the harder it is to let them go. Instead of joining forces and feeling you are on the same team, you are now fighting each other. Now he has two battles to fight: the depression and your perceptions.

Ironically, agreeing with his feelings is more likely to help. This is very different from agreeing with any dangerous action he wants to take. That you cannot do. But agreeing with his feelings is an important step. His feelings are real. They are inescapable. And they can't be wrong. It's better to say, "I don't know what to say" than to say something that puts him down or belittles his feelings. You have to be on the same side, and you have to be fighting together.

"Things could be worse."

Here, too, you think you are giving a helpful perspective, but one of the horrible things about deep depression is that perspective doesn't help. The depressed person can grasp the perspective with her mind, but in her heart, things are as bad as they can get. Logic doesn't overcome pain.

And she may hear something else. She may hear that you think she's a coward, or that you think other people would do a better job dealing with this than she is. Being thought a coward does not confer strength. Being thought strong generates strength.

You are trying to say that you have confidence in her ability to handle this. Rather than using an expression that could be misinterpreted, just come right out and say so. Be direct. Be explicit. Be clear.

In addition to not judging her, don't belittle her circumstances or her pain. She feels this is more than she can handle. For now, she is right.

"THERE'S LIGHT AT THE END OF THE TUNNEL."

Sometimes the trite sayings, the sayings one hears all the time, have the power to wound. They wound because they are supposed to be true, but the suffering person hasn't seen any sign of that yet. So in a way, your saying that "there's light at the end of the tunnel" when he hasn't seen it feels like a lie.

He may challenge you to point to something that proves there's light and that you have seen it. If you have no evidence, it will seem as if you just said something easy that came to mind. It's not that he doesn't understand how difficult it is to know what to say or that he doesn't appreciate your caring and your effort, but he's reached the point where no hope is better than false hope.

"THINGS WILL GET BETTER."

We tend to say this a lot. We may even add, "You'll see," or "It will happen." But she won't be able to see that, as much as she would like to. What she is hearing is a stock phrase. What she is feeling is a pat on the head. What she is thinking is that this applies to ordinary situations and her pain is not ordinary.

Maybe you say this every time you talk to her. Many other people may say this, too. Instead of helping, this phrase can become irritating or even infuriating. She may ask, "When?" And you won't have an answer for her. What she is realizing is that people keep saying this despite the evidence that things haven't gotten better. She doesn't want something vague; she wants something she can count on.

From her perspective, things keep getting worse. Whether her outside circumstances have changed or not, it is her internal circumstances that matter. If her ability to deal with her pain is diminishing—for whatever reason—then things are actually getting worse. When you tell her things will get better, she will see you as someone blind to reality, a misguided optimist, a weaver of fantasies. She, however, is a realist. And her choices are to fight with you—which takes up energy—or to ignore you—which also requires energy until you go away. And you don't want to deplete her energy; you want to help her generate it.

"YOU JUST NEED SOME PERSPECTIVE."

This is true, and once she has perspective, she will be able to move forward. But telling her that is not helpful. It belittles her situation and it belittles her. It says she is incapable of being rational. She knows that; it's a part of what depression is. What you, the person who cares about her, have to recognize is that her ability to understand makes her rational at the same time that reason can't help her. Inside, she is both ice cold and burning up at the same time. She is simultaneously fighting and fleeing. In other words, she is paralyzed. When one is depressed, it is both the scariest and the safest place to be.

That's what makes getting out so hard and why it feels to us as if everything we say falls on deaf ears. They hear us; they just can't listen yet. And once they can listen, they can't fully process. And once they can process, they still have to be able to act. We are very patient with our children as they learn to crawl and to walk and to talk. While someone who is depressed is relearning how to live, we need to learn a new kind of patience.

"JUST ACCEPT THINGS THE WAY THEY ARE."

Often, that's exactly the task before them, but it means giving up something else. Maybe it's faith, or belief in justice, or trust in people. Maybe it's what they always believed about how the world worked.

Maybe they have to redefine their belief system, but they may not know that's the task before them until some time goes by. Whatever propelled them to this place—outside circumstance, inner circumstance—there are stages of pain to go through. None of us can make much headway when we are consumed by emotion or completely devoid of it, and none of us can accept what *is* while railing against it. People who are depressed have a long way to go before they can reach acceptance. And we, the people who love them, need to accept that for some things, complete acceptance is never possible.

"There's nothing you can do."

You mean to tell him to accept things the way they are, to not feel guilty that he can't change things, to move forward. He may understand what you are trying to say, but it's not what he really hears. He hears: "Give up." He hears: "Everything's over." He hears: "The one thing that matters most to you, you can't do." And he hears: "You should be able to put this behind you."

What he needs is a hug—as long as he won't find it intrusive. What he needs to hear is: "You tried everything you could. There is nothing else you could have done. You did everything humanly possible." As long as that is true.

"There's always a silver lining."

In many cases, there isn't a silver lining. Often, when there is, it's only seen with hindsight, and only after years have passed.

Unless you have a particular silver lining in mind, and it's not something small or frivolous, I'd avoid sugarcoating the depression or its cause. If it is something that clearly could not balance what has happened, then you are the one who will seem to her to be irrational, or at least illogical.

WHAT ARE SOME OTHER THINGS TO AVOID SAYING?

- Don't say anything that suggests you are judging them and finding them wanting.
- Don't tell them if they did this, or said that, things would be better. Or if they had done something differently in the past, that the current situation wouldn't have happened.
- Don't get angry with them for not following your suggestions. Remember, they were suggestions, not orders. (The only exception is if you're frustrated that they have not sought evaluation or treatment when they really need it. The next chapter suggests ways to approach this.)
- Don't get upset if they can't answer your questions. For example, some people might welcome your saying, "Tell me how to help." But others might cringe. Not being able to respond is a burden. It makes them feel worse because they don't have an answer, or they don't see why they should try to think of one because "it wouldn't matter anyway."
- And don't offer unsolicited advice. The more you care about the person, the more difficult that is going to be. It is very important that they are willing to hear a suggestion and that you don't force it on them. The more one sinks into depression, the less in control one seems, the less energy one can summon to do anything, and the weaker one feels, not just physically, but mentally and emotionally. This overwhelming feeling of being depleted should *not* be reinforced.

The one exception is to urge them to get treatment, and that depends on your relationship with them and the severity of what you see. If you are a close family member or friend, or their employer, you've seen the symptoms over a period of time and they seem to be getting worse, bringing this up will be a mark of your caring.

"Hold a true friend with both your hands."

✒ Nigerian proverb

Chapter Six

Words That Work

*W*e may think we understand depression because we know what it feels like to be sad, but depression is much worse than being in the dumps. We can't fully realize this unless we come up against its horrible power. Even so, we can use what we do know. We can ask ourselves what we would like to hear if life seemed unbearable.

We would want to hear that we are not alone.

The key to providing emotional support and helping a person connect is being available to listen, and then listening in an open, accepting way. But it is not enough to simply acknowledge her feelings. It is also necessary to show empathy. Agree that her feelings are real, valid, understandable, and that they hurt. Show her you are not going to try to argue her out of them. This chapter provides examples of things you can say to help someone feel supported and respected.

"That sounds really bad. I'm sorry."

When you agree with his feelings, he will feel grateful that you accept what he has to say and that you respect it. He will feel relieved that he won't have to argue his case and will enjoy a sense of connection to another human being—you. This is wonderful because a person who is depressed often feels that no one can understand and has probably experienced other people turning away or being dismissive of his feelings. Agreeing creates an opening for words and feelings to be received. This feeling of connection is close to hope, and if it isn't yet a step forward, it can stop the step backward.

"I KNOW THIS IS GOING TO BE TERRIBLY HARD, BUT WE'LL GET THROUGH THIS NO MATTER HOW LONG IT TAKES."

Don't think that by agreeing with them you are reinforcing all the bad things: the pain, the hopelessness, the fear. You're not. You're decreasing them and providing relief. It may seem backward, but by agreeing with them you are giving them hope. Your agreement means maybe they aren't so alone after all.

But you have to keep it up for a while for that to sink in—it could take weeks or months. Eventually, when you agree with them, *they* will *disagree* with *you*. They'll feel frustrated about not moving on, they'll feel energized by your agreement, they'll rebel against it and say "enough." The wonderful thing is that they will have initiated it—and that's grounds for internal cheers. (Externally, though, be matter-of-fact about it until after the action has been carried out—maybe waiting 'til the end of the day.)

You may not see the results for a long while. You may not be able to see the relief they feel and they may not be able to tell you. But they will feel the difference between what other people say and what you say.

"YOU'RE MAKING PROGRESS AND THAT'S GREAT. YOU SHOULD BE PROUD. YOU'VE ACCOMPLISHED SO MUCH."

What energizes us? What helps us act from strength? What makes us feel strong? It's simple. Feeling strong makes us feel strong.

The person who is depressed doesn't feel strong. He feels weak, incompetent, useless, empty, drained of energy, without purpose. Nothing he could do seems worth doing. Life itself seems pointless.

Avoiding words that wound is a start; validating her feelings helps a lot. But what can help her heal is emphasizing the positive. *Not* the positives about the situation—because there may not be any—but the positives about the person. Emphasize his accomplishments, her character, his integrity, her personality, his compassion, her accomplishments, his relationships.

And get specific. Tell her in what ways she shows her character. Tell him why you hold him in such high regard. Point out facets of her personality that draw you to her. Provide examples. List the traits that make him unique. Remind her of stories in her life.

But avoid being a therapist. Many well-meaning family and friends ask probing questions. They try to analyze what's wrong, try to find the causes of the depression. Often this is what the professionals are doing. Leave that to them. Your role is rooted in the relationship you have with the person suffering from depression.

You help healing happen by being an everyday part of his life instead of an appointment, by being there out of love rather than in a professional capacity, by being an ongoing part of her life—with a history to the relationship—instead of a temporary part of her life that is there for one purpose only.

So, don't look for causes or try to pick him apart. Focus on building, reminding her of her strengths, showing your respect for his essence, and your admiration for her attitude.

Note: Sometimes the person you care about may ask you to take part in the therapeutic process. If so, the therapist will give you specific tasks to perform. Remember, you are still not the therapist, and you need to maintain the relationship you had before.

"I NEED YOUR HELP."

Try telling them what *you* need. Welcome their advice on *your* life. Welcome their assistance with practical things—setting the table, helping a child put away toys, keeping you company on an errand— and express your gratitude.

If you are feeling down yourself, let them know that. In comforting you, they may end up relieving some of their pain for a while. Let them know it is making a difference:

- "Thanks for saying that; it really helps."
- "That's a great suggestion. I'm going to do it."
- "You know, just sitting here with you helps."
- "It feels as if you understand. It takes some of the pressure off, somehow."
- "This is the best I've felt all day. I don't know how you do it, but . . ."

If they want to analyze your situation—and it's not too painful for you—let them. It will help them to help you. It will make them feel their strengths and make them experience success. It might even give them insight into their own situation. And, if nothing else, it will provide a distraction and give them some purpose.

"I'VE BEEN SO CONCERNED ABOUT YOU. A LOT OF
THINGS ARE NOT MY BUSINESS, BUT I FEEL I WOULD
BE FAILING YOU IF I DIDN'T SUGGEST THAT YOU SEE A
PROFESSIONAL. YOU'VE BEEN DOWN FOR MONTHS
NOW AND I WANT TO SEE YOU GET BETTER."

How you encourage a depressed person to seek treatment depends on
your relationship with her and the severity of what you see. Broach the
subject gently and in the form of a suggestion. Let her know that you
are not judging her—you are trying to help because you care. Point
out that if he had cancer or exhibited stroke symptoms, you would
probably have hauled him off to see someone who could assess the situation and help. If this has been going on for some time, and he seems
to be getting worse, it's okay to say that you are frustrated and that you
surely wouldn't let him walk around with a high fever for days on end
and that this seems comparable.

"HEY, YOUR ENERGY IS CATCHING. I THINK THIS TIME
YOU ARE GOING TO WEAR *ME* OUT."

People suffering from depression don't notice their own improvement,
which only adds to their discouragement. So if you notice that his
walking pace has picked up or that her face has more expression, that
he smiles sometimes or that she is talking more, or that he has more energy or she has more interest in what people are saying and doing
around her, comment on what you see. Grin back at him or listen in-
tently to her. These are encouraging and reinforcing, and they work
better than pointing out that this means they are improving, because
they are unlikely to believe that. First, it's too gradual for them to notice. Second, their perspective on themselves is too skewed for that to
make sense to them.

WHAT ARE SOME OTHER THINGS I CAN SAY THAT SHOW EMPATHY?

- "What's the worst part of this?"
- "It's hard for me to understand because I haven't been there, but I know you and respect you and hear what you say."
- "How can I help?"
- "What would you like me to do?"
- "I would be angry, too. In fact, I'm angry *for* you."
- "My heart keeps breaking for you. I am so sad, and I can't even imagine how much sadder you must be."
- "I don't know what to do except to be here. To talk when you want to talk, on any subject you like. Or to just sit here in the silence together."

Accept the silences.

WHAT ELSE CAN I SAY TO UNDERSCORE MY BELIEF IN HIM?

- "I believe in you and I believe things will get better. Because as discouraging as this is, as difficult as this is, as uncharted as this territory seems to be, other people have come through." (Mention people you know personally, or famous people who have talked about it. They would include Tipper Gore, Marie Osmond, William Styron, Mike Wallace, Sheryl Crow, and Patty Duke. Many people have written about their struggle with depression and their recovery. The Resources section lists some of these books.)
- "I believe you will get through this because you have faced this before. And because I will be here to help you get the better of this again, no matter how long it takes."

"*Words are, of course, the most powerful drug used by mankind.*"

— RUDYARD KIPLING

Chapter Seven

Dos and Don'ts

A Helpful Reference

*T*his chapter provides a cheat sheet that will help remind you of what to say and what not to say. You will probably want to put these ideas in your own words and suit them to the situation, but keep in mind that the best approach is always to be empathetic, understanding, and validating.

DON'T SAY:	DO SAY:
It's not that bad.	It sounds really bad. I'm sorry.
Things could be worse.	I wish I knew how to help.
There's light at the end of the tunnel.	We're going to get you through this. I'll help in any way I can.
Things will get better.	Call on me. Tell me what to do. I'll be there for you as long as it takes.

DON'T SAY: *(cont'd)*	DO SAY:
You know this will pass.	I love you. (Give a hug.) I'm here for you. Hang in there.
You just need some perspective.	Life can really stink. How about if we go for a walk?
Just accept things the way they are.	Some things are beyond comprehension. Beyond bearing.
There's nothing you can do.	This is the hardest thing.
There's always a silver lining.	I wish some good could come out of this, but I don't see how. There's so much pain. I hurt for you. (Hug.)
It's God's will.	You're right, this will never make sense.
It's meant to be.	It's hard to keep on believing. It will be easier when you find something to believe in again. For now, just hold on one minute at a time.
Maybe this door has to shut so another can open.	It's too soon to think about the future. It can wait. Just do what you can today. I'll help you.
This is just the way things are.	I don't know what to say, but I'm here. Three streets away. A phone call away. We're going to deal with this.

It's time you got on with your life.	You're making progress and that's okay. You should be proud. You've accomplished so much just getting to this place.
Buck up.	It's okay; this is going to take time—a lot of time.
This happens to other people. You're not the only one, you know.	This is so much worse than anything I've had to deal with. I don't know how you manage to get things done or help make things positive for others when you are in so much pain yourself.
Put it behind you and move on.	I wish it didn't have to be this way.

"Time is the longest distance between two places."

➤ TENNESSEE WILLIAMS

Chapter Eight

Answering the Unanswerable

Responding to Difficult Questions

*S*ometimes people struggling with depression will make statements that leave you with nothing to say. These are the statements you wish you had an answer to, but some have no answers. At least not answers that come in words. And not the answers a person suffering from depression really wants.

This chapter deals with statements she may make that are difficult to hear and leave us unsure of how to respond. It is meant to give you a better understanding of where she is coming from and how to reply in a way that is helpful, not hurtful.

What will he say?

- "I can't go on anymore."
- "I can't stand any more pain."
- "The pain is never going to stop."
- "There will never be a light at the end of the tunnel."
- "I hate hope."
- "I was such a coward."

At his lowest, he may be convinced that the depression will never lift, that circumstances will never change, that the right medicine will never be invented. He wants you to say, "That's not true," and he wants to believe it.

But he also wants to believe in you, so don't promise something you can't deliver. It won't help either one of you. It may be hard to stop yourself from making specific promises about what will work and when, but it's best to stick to honest answers.

Promise to be there for as long as it takes. Tell her that there are many forms of treatment and urge her to seek them out. Remind her that professionals know more than either of you about what to do. He wouldn't hesitate to see a mechanic, or a plumber, or a surgeon, or a barber, or an architect, or an accountant. This is just a different kind of expert.

WHAT PROMISES SHOULD YOU AVOID?

- "Everything is going to be all right."
- "I can fix this for you."
- "The pain will go away."
- "I know someone who can fix this for you."

WHAT CAN YOU SAY INSTEAD?

- "We don't know that."
- "I wish I knew how to take away the pain."
- "I wish I could wiggle my nose or snap my fingers and make this all right."
- "I can't fix this, but I *will* be here so you don't have to go through this alone. You can count on it."

- "You need something to hold on to. What would you like that to be? Who would you like that to be? If I'm not that person, tell me what I *can* do."
- "I don't know how to help; tell me how to help."
- "You are not a coward. You are one of the bravest people I know."
- "I know I can't possibly understand how difficult this is, but I do see you using up energy. I don't know how to help except by being here, witnessing it for you, and maybe absorbing some of it for you, too."
- "I know it's hard to imagine that it could ever get better because it has been so horrible for so long, but I believe in my heart that it won't always be like this. We just have to wait, as hard as it is to do that."

NOTE: People who say the words at the beginning of this chapter may be feeling frustrated, hopeless, or exhausted, yet they probably intend to keep on slogging through it. That is usually the case. But sometimes these words are spoken by people who are thinking of suicide. If you have even the tiniest feelings or twinges that this could be the case, go to Part 4 for suggestions on what to ask, what to say, and what to do.

Part III

What to Do

"*In music—think with the heart and feel with the brain.*"

✦ GEORGE SZELL

Chapter Nine

Without Words

USING BODY LANGUAGE TO SHOW YOUR SUPPORT

Words only convey so much. Your being there conveys a stronger message than almost anything you can say. It communicates caring, the willingness to give of your time and your energy, and that you've put other things aside because of this person's importance to you.

And sometimes words aren't appropriate. Sometimes a touch, a gesture or a facial expression will offer more. This section explores nonverbal ways to show your support. This chapter focuses on body language; the following two chapters discuss helpful actions you can take that will help the person you care about.

It is important to be aware of your body language because it can convey so much. We can all feel attitude, emotion, and judgment even when words aren't being spoken, and these could be positive or negative. Plus, when you are saying something, it is important that your body language corresponds with your words and provides additional support. Here are some things to avoid doing so you won't communicate feelings that could wound a person suffering from depression, followed by a list of things to do that will communicate your support and promote healing.

NEGATIVE SIGNALS TO AVOID:

- sarcastic, abrasive, impatient, judgmental tone of voice
- high-pitched voice
- raised voice (loud voice)
- rolling your eyes
- exchanging glances with someone else
- gritting your teeth or setting your jaw
- frowning (unless you are agreeing with them about something)
- twiddling your thumbs
- drumming your fingers on a table
- patronizing or condescending tone of voice
- talking to them as if they don't, or can't, understand what you say
- talking to them as if you were patting them on the head, as if they were children
- false jollity

POSITIVE SIGNALS THAT HELP:

- A hand on the shoulder
- Leaning toward them instead of away
- Relaxing your body
- Hugs
- Holding hands
- Putting out an arm to hold on to
- An arm around the shoulders or around the waist
- A smile
- Eye contact

- A sense of expectancy, neutrality
- An air of listening, letting them lead
- Slowing yourself down, no feeling of being rushed

To be effective at this, you have to be conscious of your negative feelings and be willing to put them aside or, better yet, transform them. Know that anger and frustration are normal, but that they won't get you anywhere. Instead, try keeping the love and respect you feel in the forefront of your mind. Set aside moments every day in which you focus on positive feelings and remember the joy and peace you have felt in their presence. With practice, you can put yourself in that place. With practice you can call upon those feelings when you are about to spend time together. And they will feel them coming from you.

But be careful that you don't start thinking of someone as a project. Always remember that no matter what the illness, it is a person you are connecting with—not a disease. No matter how worried you are, don't think of them differently, or you'll convey that to them. That sense of separation, of being different, of being diminished in your eyes, can only deepen the depression.

WHAT ACTIONS CAN YOU TAKE TO SHOW YOUR SUPPORT?

- If the person you care about would welcome it, offer to pray.
- Offer the comfort of touch. Give her a hug, a back rub or a foot massage.
- Don't be afraid to cry. Comfort each other and laugh a little at how you look afterward.
- Go on an outing: run errands, go shopping, get coffee.
- Help with a chore: clean out a closet, make dinner, pay bills.

"*We think in generalities, but we live in detail.*"

✦ ALFRED NORTH WHITEHEAD

Chapter Ten

Some Practical Support

WAYS YOU CAN HELP KEEP LIFE ON TRACK

*D*epression doesn't just affect feeling, thinking and behavior. It affects the ability to carry out the responsibilities of everyday life. This means things don't get done and may fall through the cracks. Providing practical support is another nonverbal way to help someone get through this difficult time in his life.

This kind of support is important because the person suffering from depression may not be able to accomplish necessary activities, but he knows they are there and that his situation will only get worse if he cannot carry them out. If helped with them, though, he will feel some relief. This is especially important to the person who has checked in to a hospital for a while for help. He needs to know he still has a life to go back to.

You can help with school, the job, child care, bills, and household responsibilities. Make sure that you are matter-of-fact in your approach and make sure that you consult her on how she wants them done. Try to do them in tandem. Just because she is unable to get going on them doesn't mean she doesn't know how to go about them.

Sit down with him. Make a list of what needs to be done, who needs to be called, phone numbers, and circle the date by which it should happen. Discuss the ways you can divide the responsibilities. Some tasks can be done together, like paying the bills. You open the envelopes, sort them by when they are due, consult him on which take priority, which need to be paid in full. He writes the checks, adds the stamps, and you mail them. Check back with him in a week and see if he's gotten to it yet.

Help her rally support from others. Help her figure out what to say to the kids (see chapter 16, "Tips for Kids") and ask if you could help her stay on top of their activities. You might want to help her role-play the conversations she is going to have to accomplish that.

Ask if she would like you to help her save her job. You can consult the Mental Health Association for advice on how she should handle specific workplace and related financial and legal issues. Find out where she stands on sick days and vacation leave, and whether she has disability and how it works. If she has health insurance, you could review her policy with her to see what mental-health coverage includes. But be aware that mental-health issues can still be problematic at some companies. So she will need help to find out the best person to contact, how much information to provide, the kind of questions that are appropriate, and what the ramifications might be.

If he is struggling at home, you can help there, too. Go grocery shopping together and chat as you both take care of an essential task. Get together to do paperwork at the kitchen table—you do yours, he does his. It will be easier for him to focus if you are sitting there and you may get more done yourself!

WHAT TO SAY WHEN YOU WANT TO OFFER PRACTICAL SUPPORT:

If you live together:
- "Why don't I pick up this chore for a while."
- "I'm really tired of taking out the garbage every night.

Could we switch? I'll do the bills this month and you take out the garbage?"

- "I'm having trouble getting started on this. Could you sit with me while I work on it? I don't mind if you do something else at the same time, but your sitting here might help me focus."
- "I've been looking around, and I think a lot of stuff seems to be piling up on us. You've probably noticed that too, right? Maybe we should figure out a way to get organized. Could we talk about it after dinner?"
- "I haven't had a chance to look at the mail all week and it looks kind of daunting. Could we do it together?"
- "I think we need some kind of relief around here. Which chore do you hate the most? Maybe we could trade. Or maybe we could farm something out?"
- "Are you sure you have the energy for school right now? [Pause] I was thinking that there may be some options so you don't lose all you've invested so far. Maybe there's a way for them to hold your place. Maybe you could get a leave of absence or get a refund on your tuition. Let me know if you want help researching that."
- "Do you ever get the feeling that things are getting out of control? [Pause] I want to help if I can. I know it's hard to ask for help, but I will never think less of you for asking. We're in this together. I know you would help me. In fact, you have. Please let me return the favor."
- "I know you want to get all this stuff done but you just don't have the energy to get moving these days. Why don't we figure out which things I can take over, which things we can work on together, if there's anything we can afford to farm

out for a while, and which things you can do. That way things will feel better around here, and I won't end up nudging you on everything."

- "You've been really depressed and I feel like I'm turning into a nag. I don't think that helps. Let's figure out what to do about it."

If you don't share a living space:
- "I know you've been going through a really bad patch. When that happens to me, I find myself falling behind on a lot of chores, and once they pile up, it's even more difficult to tackle them. How about I tackle one of them with you? It'll get one monkey off your back and maybe give you the momentum to tackle another one. I could get together with you on Saturday and we could split a pizza afterward."
- "I get the feeling you're getting overwhelmed lately. Maybe we could work out a deal. I help you get caught up on some things you haven't been able to get to, and sometime down the road you help me clean out a closet. I find that chore so overwhelming I can avoid it for years."
- "You know about the working woman's wish, that she could have a 'wife' to do all the daily chores? Pick up laundry. Shop for groceries. Cater dinner. Or the handyman businesses that bill themselves as a pitch-in 'husband'? Fix the leak. Build the shelves. Clean the carpets. Well, I'm offering to be that kind of 'wife' or 'husband' on a onetime basis as long as it's a chore I know how to do. This is a limited offer, so you'd better grab it now. Which one's been bugging you the most?"

- "You know, I could pitch in when you can't be in two places at once. I'll go to Joey's soccer practice while you're at Billy's tuba lesson, or do Lakeisha's car pool so you can fit in a doctor's appointment."
- "We haven't been able to get together lately and things are so busy. Would you be insulted if I suggested going grocery shopping together? Even if you don't need anything, I would love your company."
- "I know you've been having trouble getting going on things. I could be your 'nudge' factor. Call you, remind you, walk you through the steps. I've been 'nudged,' too, and there were times it really helped me."

What if she is reluctant to accept help?

- "I just want to pitch in and help you get over this hump. No point having stupid everyday stuff pile up and hang over you and drag you down."
- "Don't worry, you'll be able to return the favor someday."
- "I care about you and helping you makes me happy."

Things to keep in mind:

- The milder the depression, the more you will need to discuss and decide together. The more severe the depression, the more you'll need to just step in and say, "I'm doing this," or, "Pull the bills out and we'll deal with them this afternoon," or, "I'm here to clear this out of the way for you"—the more likely it will be that you will do these things for her rather than with her.

- If the person you are helping lives with someone, such as a spouse, make sure he or she is comfortable about your helping with things around the house, or with children, or with financial, medical, legal or insurance matters.
- If the person you are helping has older children, don't take away responsibilities they want to keep or want to undertake.

"She is a friend of my mind. . . . The pieces I am, she gather them and give them back to me in all the right order."

✒ FROM *BELOVED* BY TONI MORRISON

Chapter Eleven

Gifting

What You Can Give to Help Healing Happen

*T*he greatest gift you can give people who are suffering from depression is to help them retrieve themselves: their identity, their self-respect, their dreams, their self-confidence, their humor, and their sense of connection. Let them know that you still see these things in them and it will help them see these things in themselves.

When you give them back themselves, you are not just giving them your love, you are restoring their energy and refueling their strength. When the person reemerges, the depression submerges, and vice versa. It may not be entirely gone, but it will no longer be so savagely in control.

How do you do this? By giving them the gift of yourself: your time, your energy, your presence; your love, your admiration and your patience. Most important, your mutuality—by letting them know that this is still a relationship between peers.

Two concrete ways in which we can do this are by giving them something tangible or by involving them in action. They both have the same goal: to help them reconnect with what is strong and beautiful in themselves, other people, and the world, and to reawaken possibilities and capabilities. This chapter suggests specific gifts you might give.

Sometimes giving a tangible gift helps. Something that can be touched or experienced with other senses. Something that is still there when you are not, and it doesn't have to cost money.

It can be a simple object or something made of words. Up to now the focus of this book has been on the words we can say aloud, in the moment, with immediacy. But words can be very powerful when they are written down—when they can be seen, held with our hands, made somehow more solid and permanent. Here are some things you can give—with words, without words.

THE GIFT THEY CAN HOLD

- Something you bake, or soup for the freezer.
- Flowers from the garden.
- A handkerchief with your scent.
- A sweater she loves on you that she can wear.
- Your tie.
- A cutting from a plant he is drawn to.
- A bowl from the dishes she admires in your kitchen.
- A picture a child has drawn.
- A polished stone to hold; a kaleidoscope to turn; a stuffed animal to stroke.
- A letter telling him how much he means to you, how you admire him, how he has helped you, how much you look forward to similar occasions or a special occasion you plan to experience with him.
- A favorite book from his childhood.
- A book with a character you admire that reminds you of her with a note telling her that in the flyleaf of the book. She'll

read the book to tease out what you mean and appreciate being shown this side of herself.

- If she is severely depressed and has difficulty reading, you could point out the inscription as you hand her the book and read it aloud. You could mention some of the ways the character reminds you of her, and tell her those are things you admire about her.

- Ask him to get out paper and pen and write down what you are about to say, then start telling him all the things you admire about him and why. He will own the message as his fingers form the words, and he'll be able to pull out those pages whenever he needs to remind himself of who he is. And you can do this over the phone, too.

- Send supportive e-mails, cards, messages on answering machines and voice mail, notes you drop off. Not only can these be looked at over and over again, but they can be looked at in his own time. And they don't require him to interact with you.

THE GIFT OF SPONTANEITY

Make a list of activities you can do together or things he can do on his own. It can be simply formatted, just words on paper, or you can get creative and make a coupon book. This will offer specific choices and invite her to pick up the phone and set an activity in motion.

Here's a list of suggestions:

- crying jag
- screaming session
- getting a manicure
- game of tennis

- going bowling
- a jog or a run
- going out for ice cream
- a card game
- bingo
- a walk in the park
- a massage
- a foot rub
- going to tag sales
- rearranging the furniture
- gripe session
- gossip fest
- meeting for coffee
- going out for breakfast
- meeting for dinner
- visit to a museum
- attending a concert
- renting a video
- going to a movie
- making homemade ice cream
- watching a ball game on television together
- going to a baseball game (for sports fans, list games separately)
- ordering pizza
- ordering Chinese
- going to a rehearsal
- making nachos and cheese
- playing a board game (for people who love games, list these separately)

- going shopping
- painting a room
- starting a jigsaw puzzle; leave it out to work on daily
- getting hair done together
- attending a community event—fair, festival, meeting
- setting up a '50s night (or some other decade); singing old songs
- making music together; impromptu band
- cleaning out a closet or a drawer
- visiting someone together
- going to a craft show
- going to a flower shop
- visiting a zoo
- rereading a favorite book
- introducing a favorite book to a friend

THE GIFT OF WORDS

Some of us aren't verbal; we freeze or think we're not good at putting words down on paper when it involves emotions. I can't tell you how many people in my life ask me to review something they've written before they send it, or ask for help in drafting it. These are intelligent, competent people who write well in other areas but have no confidence in this one. If this is the case, the samples below might help.

You might write short notes that can be tucked in envelopes, under pillows, in lunch boxes, in briefcases, in coat pockets, or left on the kitchen table.

SHORT NOTES CAN SAY:

- "Being with you just lifts me up."
- "Without you I'm toast."
- "You're brave and beautiful."
- "How proud I am of you."
- "You're the best."
- "Many people couldn't do what you do."
- "You fight a real battle every day and find the strength to do that over and over."
- "You are an extraordinary person."
- "You are so genuine."
- "No one is as caring and kind as you are."
- "I love you more every day."
- "You're so kissable."
- "How about a movie after work?"

HERE'S A SAMPLE LETTER:

"I am the person I am because of you. I have always admired you so much—your persistence, your strength, your sense of responsibility. Most of all I've treasured your friendship. You've always been there. To listen. To help. To laugh with me. To ground me when things were spinning out of control. I'd never have survived being a teenager without you. We've weathered so many things through the years. We'll weather this, too. Together."

THE GIFT OF ACTIVITY

It is not only *our* actions that count, it is theirs. Anything we can do to help people with depression focus intensely on something else, really feel something with their five senses, feel action or creativity flowing through their bodies, or have a sense of having acted positively on a person or the world, will help to shift the way they experience their own thoughts.

The following suggestions are reminders of commonplace activities that can make a difference, together with a discussion of what makes them powerful and how they work. There are eight categories. Keep in mind, though, that the more severe the depression, the more effort will be required to even try. Getting him started—especially by joining him in some of these activities—can help make it happen and give them the chance to work.

Help someone else

For many people, the most powerful medicine is the feeling of helping someone else. When we help someone, even in the smallest way, we see that we can make a difference. We see that we can act upon the world; it's not just the world that acts on us.

One of the hallmarks of depression is a feeling of helplessness, hopelessness, and worthlessness. The idea of giving of oneself when one feels one has nothing to give may seem strange, but that is the best time to give. Because other people are always giving to the person suffering from depression, he is always the receiver. Feeling increasingly dependent on others won't help him.

Find a way for him to be the giver, not the receiver, or point out to him where he is giving and may not realize it. Help him help someone else and then help him do it again. It's like filling an account with deposits drop by drop. Drops of strength, self-confidence, and self-worth.

It is very difficult for someone who is giving of himself on a regular basis to follow through on suicidal thoughts. Someone else's need can be grounding, absorbing and compelling. It is precisely because he feels abandoned and betrayed that he cannot abandon and betray someone else.

SING

To the Greeks, singing was a panacea for emotional turbulence, a cure-all. It can't really achieve that, but it will get oxygen into the lungs, blood to the extremities, and words and sounds shaped by lips and tongue and lungs and larynx. It's tough to do at first, but it comes back. It engages the senses and the body and the mind. His ears may feast on the sound, his feet may tap to the beat, and someone else may join in. You might put on music, or you could sing together, or he could sing alone. Help him join a choir, pick up an instrument, join a band, start a chamber music group, make music with children.

WORK

To the Romans, work was healing. At first work may just be a distraction, a way to fill up one's thoughts and push away pain. But the act of moving forward, accomplishing tasks and achieving results all symbolize having areas of influence in which one can take charge and exert some control. There is a momentum to any kind of continuous, consistent activity that can spill over into other areas of one's life. Logic cannot conquer pain and action cannot do so either, but it can help to put it in a box temporarily, to keep it out of the foreground of the picture some of the time and give one's constant attention to it a respite.

CONNECT

A person can connect to other people by working together, singing to-gether, dancing together, through touch, and by consciously breathing the same air. Encourage him to interact with people he doesn't know. Reengaging with people you know is harder so it can come later. In-stead, start with situations that don't require much conversation, in which she won't feel put on the spot, in which there will be no expecta-tions for her to say or do anything, and which she can easily leave early. She might attend a sporting event, parade, church, or a general meeting. She can go on her own, or with someone like you who is flexible, easy-going, and won't mind ducking out early and calling it a day. She can take it in stages, build up to things slowly, and give herself a safety zone.

Why does this work? Because a stranger won't know about his de-pression, or how he used to be, or anything else about him. This makes smiling at a stranger easier than smiling at someone he knows. Many strangers—whether they suffer from depression or not—will feel the same. They will feel pleasantly surprised and smile back. And they won't expect conversation. This is a way to connect without probing, a way to connect without having to say how one feels or if one is feeling better, a connection without having to provide a progress report. The boundaries are clear; the exchange doesn't take much energy; and it is short. Any public place will do for this: the per-son next to her in line, the cashier at the grocery store, the person walking out of a building when he is walking in.

CREATE

There are so many ways to create, and so many ways to define creating. Creating any kind of art, music, stories, poems, sewing, crocheting, craft work, gardening, designing, or metalwork is helpful. Getting involved in the process of creating is what makes the difference, more so than the product. Some projects lend themselves to biting off just one manageable chunk at a time. Crocheting an afghan out of squares is a good example; one can create a square in a few minutes, and gradually build up to the completed blanket one square at a time. Helping out at a nursery school or a senior center where someone is in charge of crafts and could use an extra pair of hands can be rewarding, too. One can end up participating in all kinds of crafts one would never have thought of.

Exercise

Exercise reduces stress, increases serotonin, and makes one feel stronger. Even just a ten-minute walk can make a difference. Plan to go walking with her for a few weeks to get a routine going. Once it becomes a habit, she will be less likely to stop because she will be more likely to miss it. Exercise adds structure to the day, too. The rest of the day becomes "before" and "after." If she hasn't exercised for a long time, or just can't get going, start with simple breathing exercises and light stretching. Marathons are not required.

Make small changes

It could be in his surroundings. Redecorate by picking up one new pillow, one new throw, moving the furniture, putting up a new picture, different napkins. It could be in a process. Renavigate by creating a new route to drive somewhere she goes all the time. It could be in her appearance. Help her pick out a new hairstyle, a new clothing style, or add one small distinctive change—a scarf, a belt, wearing blues instead of greens, browns instead of grays, retiring favorite earrings in favor of a new pair, wearing new glasses. It could also be in the ambiance. Renew the senses by changing furniture polish, trying a different toothpaste, using a new shampoo, adding potpourri or subtracting it, switching perfumes, or trying a new coffee flavor each week. The person you care about could also change the way he normally does things. He could create a new ritual by adding a course to dinner (it could be a cheese course, or a salad course, or a dessert course). She might add something to the going-to-bed ritual such as a cup of tea before bed, or a particular piece of music, or writing down the dream she'd like to have that night.

These small changes are positive acts that get immediate results and produce long-term benefits. They are easy to institute, they offer choices, and they make her feel she has some control over what happens. But the most important thing they do is make her environment—what she experiences with her senses—feel different. This expands the world beyond a place that might have been associated with pain. The more she makes small changes, the sooner the big changes will come. At first, it's best to take a lot of little ones all in isolation and not to raise expectations at all.

MAINTAIN A ROUTINE

Structuring our day by getting up at the same time and eating our meals at the same time helps us mentally and physically. It affects the very chemistry of our bodies and our brains. We have all kinds of internal clocks that release enzymes and hormones to regulate when we are hungry, when we are sleepy, when we are fertile, when our energy peaks and when it dips. The importance of these internal clocks to our general well-being becomes obvious when we travel to another time zone. Everything gets thrown off: waking up, being able to sleep, appetite, digestion, energy, moods, ability to be alert, to think clearly. It often takes a few days for most people to adjust and then to feel at home in one's skin again.

If he is depressed and can't get out of bed, can't fall asleep, forgets to eat, or starts eating all the time, he will have thrown his clocks off. Anything you can do to help him get back in kilter will be a plus. It won't take away the depression, but it will help him function better and even feel a little better. One needs all the energy one can get and all the strength one can muster to deal with this thing. Help him make his body work *for* him.

Another thing that helps all of us get up in the morning is having a place we need to be or having something to do that can't go undone. For most of us that's work or getting a child off to school. It's incredibly hard to be motivated even by these things when in the grip of depression, but it would be even harder to get out of bed if those things weren't there. So make sure there's a place she has to be and some way to get her there. The more structure she has in her life, the more there is to hold on to.

Part IV

SUICIDE

"A friend is a second self."

✄ ARISTOTLE

Chapter Twelve

Warning Signs

WHAT TO LOOK FOR

*W*hen dealing with depression, the most dangerous risk is suicide. It isn't always easy to predict when a depressed person is considering suicide, but there are telltale warning signs. This section explores ways to respond when you are afraid someone you care about is considering suicide. The first chapter goes over some warning signs and the next chapter explores ways to talk to someone who might be suicidal.

THE AMERICAN ASSOCIATION OF SUICIDOLOGY LISTS THESE WARNING SIGNS OF SUICIDE:

- Talks about committing suicide
- Has trouble eating or sleeping
- Experiences drastic changes in behavior
- Withdraws from friends and/or social activities
- Loses interest in hobbies, work, school, etc.
- Prepares for death by making out a will and final arrangements
- Gives away prized possessions

- Has attempted suicide before
- Takes unnecessary risks
- Has had recent severe losses
- Is preoccupied with death and dying
- Loses interest in their personal appearance
- Increases their use of alcohol or drugs

SAVE, THE SUICIDE AWARENESS/VOICE OF EDUCATION ORGANIZATION, INCLUDES THESE ADDITIONAL DANGER SIGNS:

- Suddenly happier, calmer
- Visiting or calling people one cares about
- Statements about hopelessness, helplessness, or worthlessness

One of the things that makes this difficult to predict is that some behaviors can be interpreted more than one way. His sudden lift in spirits and energy could come from a lifting of the depression (in which case you would rejoice) or it could come from his relief at having made a final decision (in which case you should be worried). Her suddenly getting organized—cleaning out files, cleaning out closets, cleaning house—could signal an effort to take a small measure of control (which would be a step forward) or it could signal her putting her house in order for those she would leave behind (which could worry you even more).

It helps to have some information about his family background, his medical history, or what has been going on recently with her medications.

You should know if:

- She has attempted suicide before
- Someone else in his family has committed suicide
- He stopped taking medications
- She just changed medications
- His treatment plan and how he's doing in general haven't been assessed for a while
- Her meds are always having to be adjusted (and this is not usual for her)
- He has become very anxious and agitated (This tends to make people act impulsively; getting help with these will lower the risk of suicide.)

There are two other warning signs to be aware of that may indicate suicide, both of which may lead you to relax and think things are under control when you need to be vigilant:

Her medications may have just *started working*

For someone who suffers from moderate to severe depression, the point when medications *start* making a difference is a time to watch. Normally, you'd think, "That's great! His medications are kicking in, and things are going to get better." But things aren't in sync yet, and this can be a dangerous period. Depression saps energy to such an extent that even if someone wants to commit suicide, he may not be able to summon up the energy to do it. Medications will help to lift the depression, but they tend to work in stages. They tend to affect energy first, mood second, so she will get back her energy *before* her mood changes, and that puts her at risk. For those first few days or weeks, she may still want to commit suicide, and now she has the energy to act.

He's bipolar, and seems happy

When the person you care about suffers from bipolar disorder, things are contrary to what you might expect. The layperson tends to get scared when the person she cares about is in the depressive phase, but the underlying depression is still very much present in the manic phase and in what is called a "mixed state"—when he seems to be in neither but is really transitioning. To you, it looks like he is up, full of energy, vitality, plans and action. But this is the time he is most likely to be impulsive, reckless, and likely to put his life in danger. It's the energy that makes action possible, so that is when someone with bipolar disorder is at greatest risk.

One of the most reliable warning signs of all is your gut feelings. Don't ignore them—you may be processing information subconsciously that you are not consciously aware of. If you are scared, you need to act immediately. If your gut tells you things are very wrong, call a doctor, a crisis center, the person's therapist, 911, or head for the emergency room. And don't leave him or her alone.

"You cannot do a kindness too soon,
for you never know how soon it will be too late."

➤ RALPH WALDO EMERSON

Chapter Thirteen

Assessing Imminent Danger

WHAT TO ASK

*W*hen you suspect that someone is suicidal, the best thing you can do is ask them about it. Don't worry about planting the idea in her head or pushing her to act if she has been hesitating. Instead, asking shows that you care and are committed to helping her. Chances are she is scared of her own thoughts and will be relieved to have some help. This chapter lists ways to ask and how to respond if the person is suicidal.

WHAT TO ASK:

- "Are you going to be all right?"
- "Are you thinking about taking your life?"
- "Are you thinking about hurting yourself?"
- "Do I have to worry that you are going to do something to-night?"
- "I need to ask you something. Will you make it through the night?"
- "You sound particularly low. Please tell me if you're planning to do anything."

- "You sound particularly low. Can I count on you not to do anything tonight?"
- "Are you planning on hurting yourself?"
- "Do you feel you are going to kill yourself tonight?"

WHEN THE ANSWER IS "YES"

Don't panic if the answer is "yes." Get some clarification:

- "What are you thinking?"
- "Do you have a plan?"
- "How are you planning to do it?"
- "When are you thinking of doing it?"

If she has a plan and a timetable, ask if she has the means to carry it out. If she says no, the threat may not be immediate. You can show your love by insisting that one of you call the person he sees for counseling *immediately*. That person can't talk to *you* (for patient confidentiality reasons), but you can talk to *her* and she can listen.

If he does not have a therapist, urge him to get an evaluation. Offer to make an appointment for him with someone who can assess the situation. Realize that this may lead to hospitalization. If the person you care about is willing to make that call himself and take the responsibility of asking for help, it will be a voluntary admission and he will be free to leave when he wants unless professionals feel he is an immediate danger to himself or others. If he refuses to make the call himself, and you or his therapist feel he is in danger, then it could lead to an involuntary commitment. This is a very difficult call.

How to encourage help:

- "You're scaring me. Please consider getting some therapy, or counseling, or something."
- "What you are saying scares me and I want you alive tomorrow."
- "You're scaring me. I want you to call your therapist."
- "You're scaring me. If you don't call your therapist, I will."
- "You're scaring me. And I think you're scaring yourself, too. I think you should call your therapist or check yourself in."
- "You must do one or the other—call or check yourself in."
- "Who's going to make the call? You or I?"

If she is in immediate danger

If it is an emergency, call the local crisis hotline (the number will be in the phone book) or go to the hospital emergency room. If she has a plan, a timetable, and the means—call 911.

And don't wait for an emergency to look up phone numbers and addresses. Prepare yourself to do this by asking for the name and phone number of the therapist just in case and by calling the local crisis hotline for advice ahead of time—explain that you need advice in order to help someone you care about and ask them to guide you through the process. Make sure that the person you care about knows you are prepared to do this by having a conversation about it with him before an emergency happens. This emotionally prepares both of you for your interfering in this way, and it makes it possible for you to preserve your relationship if the phone call has to be made.

We tend to worry that calling the therapist is overreacting, but it's much better to have an angry live friend than a dead one. She may talk suicide and then insist that she's okay and will call you in the morning, but she may not be able to live up to that. She doesn't really trust her own ability to act or follow through right now, so you may not be able to rely on her words, either.

WHY NOT JUST CALL 911 RIGHT AWAY?

- Because it's always a good idea to assess the situation before reacting.
- It might not be an emergency.
- The person you care about might be willing to get help on a nonemergency basis.
- This might be an ongoing situation in which warning signs appear every few days or weeks. You don't want to become jaded or desensitized to them—you absolutely have to take them seriously each and every time—but you also don't want to cry wolf.

That being said, it is always better to err on the side of caution. If your gut says this is it, or you've been in this position before and you feel a lot more leery than usual, make the call.

WHY IS ASKING THESE QUESTIONS SO HARD?

You're afraid of intruding, of being wrong, of losing a friendship. You can't figure out what to say and you don't know what you'll do with the answers. But whether you are a family member or friend, the more experience you have with asking these questions, the easier it will get. The situation will never get easier, but your ability to ask the questions will because you'll know they come out of love. If the people you care about can't see that right away, they'll see it later. And that later may exist because of you.

If you haven't done it before, your questions may be tentative. That's okay. Just don't back off. Ask all the questions, persist through intent, timetable, and means, then reach a conclusion and act on it.

If you've had to do this before, no matter how scared and frustrated you are that someone you love keeps coming back to this place, ask the questions with love. Keep anger out of your voice, but be resolute and prepared to follow through.

WHAT KIND OF RESISTANCE SHOULD I EXPECT?

- Anger.
- Telling you to back off.
- Telling you they are fine.
- Asking you to just let them get on with it.
- Asking you to promise to keep this to yourself.

Listen, but don't promise secrecy because it could make it impossible for you to get them the help they need. Their survival and well-being override everything else.

WHAT IF HE'S IN DANGER AND I'M FAR AWAY?

You might be a parent whose child is away at school, a sister who lives in another state, a friend tied down who can't get there. Whether you can get there or not, you can ask these questions and arrange for someone else to show up if you can't be there yourself. You don't have to be physically present to ask these questions or to call a crisis center. The important thing is to be sure they are not alone.

"*Friendship with oneself is all-important*

🕊 ELEANOR ROOSEVELT

Chapter Fourteen

Still Here

Moving Toward Survival

*M*any people beat back the compulsion to attempt suicide. Of those who do attempt it, some survive and some don't. This chapter talks about the strength of all those haunted by thoughts of suicide, and it talks about the strength of those of us who do our best to help them fight it.

People suffering from depression are survivors. They face indescribable pain every day. They fight the terror of the pain never ending and fight the only logical way out of that pain. That takes extraordinary willpower and strength. It often takes all their reserves of energy not just not to think about suicide, but not to act on the relief it promises. To them, ending their lives would mean ending the pain.

When pain is unceasing, relentless, and unbearable, it is not only the mind that reaches a conclusion. The body is drawn to that conclusion as a lodestar is driven toward the poles. The mind may reach that conclusion dispassionately and neutrally; the body is pulled to it as if it were an irresistible force. It is the mind that also makes the decision not to act, so the mind must fight both itself and the body.

Many people suffering from depression survive suicide every day.

Literally. They survive the impulse to act, and this can be a burning, overwhelming and repeated desire.

People suffering from depression are strong and resilient and brave. We don't see it because the battle is not visible, but that doesn't mean we can't recognize it and acknowledge it. This battle takes place inside, and it rages in silence.

We admire people who are brave, who achieve staggering feats in the face of mind-boggling obstacles. These survivors of suicide may look wrung out, incapable of making decisions, unable to exert themselves physically, but they are among the bravest people we know. We need to tell them that we see that. We need to tell them how brave they are and how we admire them for it. We need to tell them that their strength inspires us and assure them that we will do what we can to help them renew their reserves of energy and shore up their strength.

We need to remind them of how strong they are because they may be absorbing other people's assessments. We tend to internalize what other people think of us, even if they never say their thoughts out loud. Facial expressions, tones of voice, and avoidance can all convey a negative opinion. If other people think we are weak, or lazy, or ineffectual, or giving up, we will come to believe it of ourselves, and that will weaken us and diminish us.

Don't let that happen to the people you care about. They are fighting the toughest battles, and only strength and courage can help them prevail. Remind them that it is their own strength and courage that is doing the job, and that that is how you see them.

No matter how strong people are, no matter how courageous, not everyone makes it. If the person you care about acts on their suicidal thoughts, you will grieve, feel anger, feel guilt, wonder what else you might have done, wonder if what you did was worth it.

Please know that nothing will change the value of what you do.

What you do can make a difference by enhancing the quality of her days, extending the time during which medication and therapy can take effect, and increase the chances for recovery. This isn't to say that you can make *the* difference. There are just too many factors involved.

If the person you care about acts on his suicidal thoughts, you are not responsible for that act. You are not omniscient or omnipotent. You are doing your best and he is ultimately responsible. Whether something else you could have done would have changed it is unknowable, and it is very self-destructive to dwell there.

It is also self-destructive to think that he doesn't love you enough to keep going. Many are helped in these battles by the love they feel for other people in their lives, and the love those people feel for them. That connection can often help them pull back from suicide, but sometimes the pain will overwhelm that connection, swamp the love, sap the energy and willpower needed to give up the relief that would come with ending everything. But this has to do with their pain, not with their love.

Thinking of her as a coward is also destructive. Some battles are harder than others. Sometimes, after so many prior battles, there just aren't enough reserves of energy to transform strength and courage into action. Sometimes, one is just overwhelmed by the enemy. In physical battles, we celebrate the bravery of the soldier who falls. The bravery of the psychological warrior is no less.

What you do can change the quality of his life, and sometimes help him keep going until he's past the horrible bump or hole that is skewering him to where he is. You do that by boosting his bravery, because none of us can live in a continuous state of courage.

Helping her move in a positive direction through acceptance, validation, love, respect, distraction, purpose, and a shift in behavior and thought process—this is what you can aim for.

Part V

LIVING DAY TO DAY

*"The trouble with being poor
is that it takes up all your time."*

— WILLEM DE KOONING

Chapter Fifteen

Situation by Situation

One Thing at a Time

No matter what your degree of involvement, you will run into situations you are not sure how to handle, which can be unnerving. This chapter is meant to prepare you for specific situations you may encounter. It is organized in question-and-answer format like the FAQ section at the beginning of this book, but instead of providing general information about depression, it pinpoints specific situations that often come up. The key is to take it day by day and handle each situation as it comes—and no matter what the circumstances, to always approach each situation with sensitivity.

He seems down. How do I broach the subject?

It depends on how well you know him and on how down he seems, and you might want to bring it up gradually over a period of weeks. If you don't know him well, you may want to approach him in passing at first. Either way, just make a simple observation and wait a little to see if he responds. Don't push it. Say it matter-of-factly or with a slight question in your voice. If he doesn't respond, let the subject drop. But if he still doesn't look right over the next couple of weeks, and it feels right to you, try taking him aside and letting him know what you've noticed. Be prepared for silence at first, or something dismissive.

The best approach is to be direct. Let her know in a matter-of-fact way that something seems wrong and you are concerned about her. It might be helpful to mention something specific because it may be something she didn't realize herself. For example, maybe she stopped coming to book-club meetings, or he stopped coming to the poker game, or she started showing up late for work, or he stopped going to services.

You might say:

- "You look a little tired. I hope everything's okay."
- "You look a little down. I hope you don't mind me asking, but is everything okay?"
- "You don't look yourself. What's happening?"
- "You just haven't sounded like yourself the last few times we talked. What's wrong?"
- "I get the feeling something's wrong. Do you want to talk about it? Can I help?"
- "If something's wrong, and there's something I can do to help, I hope you'll tell me."
- "This friendship is for good times and bad. It'd hurt my feelings if you didn't take advantage of that when the going gets rough."
- "I know you'd be there for me; please let me be there for you."

DEPENDING ON THE REPLY, YOU COULD FOLLOW UP WITH:

- "I'm sorry to hear that. Is there anything I can do?"
- "I'm sorry to hear that. Would it help if I . . . [offer something specific]"
- "If it would help to talk about it, I would be glad to listen."
- "I hope I didn't intrude. I just hope everything is okay. I think you're a great person, and it just seemed to me something was on your mind."
- "I don't want to pry, but I've been worried. I noticed that [mention something she is doing differently, or not doing at all]. If it turns out there's something I can help with, even if it's just to talk, I'm here."

WHAT IF HE KEEPS PUTTING ME OFF?

If he keeps putting you off, try treating him to something. Something small, something silly, something in the nature of an inside joke, something that symbolizes him or something you've done together. It could be cookies or brownies, a T-shirt with a saying he'd appreciate, a mug with an appropriate motto, a cartoon that fits his philosophy, a comic strip that suits his funny bone, tickets to a movie, a bag of microwave popcorn with a gift certificate to a video store, a homemade coupon for a day doing something with you that you know he'd love to do. Present it in an offhand way. Say, "Just wanted to let you know I'm thinking of you," or "For some reason, this had your name on it."

He may not be ready to open up and talk about it, but he'll know you care and will feel more comfortable about confiding in you at a later time.

WHAT IF I'M WRONG? WHAT IF HE'S OKAY? HOW CAN I TELL IF IT'S WORTH PURSUING?

You can only go on gut feel, which is based on your many observations of a particular person over a period of time. This is often very difficult. You certainly don't want to take any kind of drastic action—or even keep bugging someone about feeling down—if he really has things under control. On the other hand, if someone you care about really needs help, you can't in good conscience do nothing.

The best thing to do is look for warning signs or changes in behavior and ask him about them. If the person won't acknowledge that there is a problem, you could consider talking to him about your concerns.

You can ask:

- "There's something I'd like to talk to you about. Could you give me a couple of minutes after work?"
- "This is really awkward, and I know you haven't encouraged my asking you about this, but I need to explain where I'm coming from. I've faced something like this before and I've regretted not saying anything. If this is a similar situation, I don't see how I can walk away. Please, I don't need to know your business, but would you tell me a way I can help you?"
- "If you can't reach out for your own sake, would you do it for me? Would you do it for your family?"
- "Have you had a physical recently? Maybe a checkup would be worth having."

WHAT IF SHE'S SUFFERED FROM DEPRESSION IN THE PAST AND IT LOOKS LIKE IT'S STARTING TO HAPPEN AGAIN?

Bring it to her attention. Tell her you are seeing some of the behaviors you saw last time and you think she may be spiraling down so gradually she might not have realized it. If she was in treatment before, ask her if she's seen her therapist lately. If she was taking medications, ask her if she is still taking them or if she has had them adjusted recently. Suggest she get reevaluated. Remind her that the medical community's knowledge is constantly evolving and that intervening quickly may save her a lot of suffering.

It's easier to have this conversation if you have talked about the possibility of a recurrence beforehand and discussed the ways you could help if there ever was a next time.

The timing of intervention can matter because it's easier to climb partway up a hill than to have to climb all the way from the bottom. So, if the two of you (or a group of friends and family members) can pinpoint the early warning signs, speak up. If she can address the problem sooner, then emergencies could be avoided, the depth of the depression might be shallower, and its length shorter.

You can also set up a code word. It's good to have a shorthand way of taking his "mental temperature" without having to get into a discussion, and it's discreet if overheard when talking on the phone or at the job. It's a way to sound an alarm—"I'm in trouble" or getting close to it. And it isn't as emotionally taxing as asking and answering probing questions.

A scale of one to ten is the simplest way to do this. All you'd have to do is say, "What's today's number?" and no one else would need to know what that means. Or another gradation scale could be used, such as A to Z, or an analogy to something in life such as swimming. He might be treading water, sinking, drowning, or going under.

Another way to be supportive is to recognize that, for some people, depression is recurrent because it is part of their body chemistry. It can have flare-ups that need to be treated and there is nothing that anyone did that caused them; they just happen on their own.

WHAT IF I THINK HIS GRIEF HAS TURNED INTO DEPRESSION?

Encourage him to go for depression screening and offer to make the appointment for him. There are also grief support groups—offer to find one for him in your community. Sometimes the griever can connect best with strangers who are in the same place or who have been there recently but are now doing better. For more information on distinguishing grief from depression, see chapter 1. For more information on getting a preliminary screening, see the Resources section.

WHAT IF I TALK TO HER ABOUT IT AND SHE DENIES THERE IS A PROBLEM?

Unless you think she's a danger to herself or others, there's not much you can do directly. Just be there, be a friend. Suggest doing things together, call her; if you have close mutual friends, enlist their support. Maybe that will keep her going for a while until she can come to one of you and ask for help.

HE SUFFERS FROM DEPRESSION, BUT ACTS HAPPY ALL THE TIME. WHAT DOES THIS MEAN AND WHAT SHOULD I DO?

Sometimes, when we're running a fever, or our bodies hurt for some other reason, we feel so tender that we shy away from any physical touch. Sometimes, minds and hearts can't bear to be touched either. They flinch from any real contact.

People suffering from depression may use happiness as a barrier to keep us at a distance so emotional wounds can't be probed and can start to form scar tissue. This sends us a signal that even acknowledging the pain is more than they can bear, and it lets us know that a pretense of normalcy, for now, is their way of holding on to sanity when nothing makes sense.

When someone you care about acts happy all the time, yet you know the person is depressed and has reason to be, you will have to walk a tightrope as much as he is doing. He needs to act as if everything is fine so people won't "pick" at him, yet he doesn't really want those closest to him to assume that everything is fine, he is cured, and no one need worry about him or provide emotional support any longer.

Your balancing act is to respect the barrier yet at the same time to convey your respect, your understanding, and your availability. One way of doing that subtly is to hold his hand a little longer when you clasp it, give him a hug or pat on the back, say, "call me whenever." If you don't hear from him in a couple of days, call him to say hello. You could also try sharing your own problems with him. Sometimes, that can help the other person open up.

SHE'S ALWAYS BEEN HEALTHY, BUT SHE SEEMS TO BE BECOMING A HYPOCHONDRIAC. SHOULD I WORRY?

Aches and pains that won't go away, or that keep cropping up in one part of the body after the other, could be signs of a physical illness and should be checked out by a doctor. But if the doctor can't find any physical cause, they could also be a sign of depression, and either you or the doctor should encourage checking this out, too. Getting an evaluation could make the difference between getting treatment and getting worse.

HE HADN'T INVITED ME OVER FOR A WHILE, AND I JUST CAN'T BELIEVE THE MESS. HIS HOME WAS NEVER LIKE THAT. WHAT SHOULD I DO?

Sometimes people can maintain a great façade at work and in short encounters but are almost nonfunctional at home. Though this is not on the list of symptoms listed in the first chapter, it is a result of some of them and is something a layperson can easily see. If you notice that his home is very different from the way it looked before, that everything seems to be falling apart, and realize it had to take time to get that way, there may be reason for concern. It's a tip-off to look closely to see if he has any other symptoms of depression.

WHAT IF SHE IGNORES ALL MY ADVICE?

This is frustrating, but it is okay. The whole world is probably burying her in advice every day and she has no energy left to decide what advice to take, much less the energy she might need to act on it.

It isn't her job to listen to you; it's your job to listen to her. That's the best way to help her. Listen, and she'll feel connected and loved. Listen, and she'll have a chance to unburden herself, a chance to think aloud and maybe plan. And you might remember some things she used to like to do and be able to remind her of them.

The only time for you to worry about advice not taken is if you think she is in immediate danger of harming herself or someone else. Then you must act (see chapter 13).

HE CAN'T GET HIMSELF OUT OF BED IN THE MORNING. HOW SHOULD I RESPOND?

Many people struggling with depression sleep a lot. It's not just an escape, it's entering a realm that's restorative. But if he stays in bed most of the day, every day, you should be concerned—if he is not receiving professional help, urge him to go for depression screening right away. If he is in treatment, encourage him to let his doctor know because this may be a sign that the depression is worsening. In the meantime, know that the extra sleep itself isn't harming him. Sleep doesn't remove what is causing the depression, but it does slow the drain of energy and give our internal reservoirs a chance to replenish themselves.

You can also offer to be her human alarm clock and give her a wake-up call each morning. If this isn't possible, suggest she use a backup alarm clock or set up a regular early-morning meeting—coffee, a jog, a walk—with someone she wouldn't want to stand up, and offer to be one of those people.

SHE GOES TO BED LATER AND LATER. HOW SHOULD I RESPOND?

People with depression often function better later in the day. This makes for later bedtimes, because if there are things that need doing, it may be past bedtime before she has the energy and self-discipline to do them.

She also may be going to bed later and later to increase the chances that she'll fall asleep right away. Going to bed can mean that her mind will take over and her thoughts will go round and round and prevent her from sleeping, so she wants to be as tired as possible before going to bed. Or she may be someone who tends to wake up early every morning—say at 4 A.M.—and can never get back to sleep. This is very common among people suffering from depression, and seems to happen no matter when they go to bed.

No matter what group she belongs to, she'll have difficulty getting up in the morning and functioning during the day, because she will never feel rested, refreshed or alert.

You can help by sitting up with her, or encouraging her to set up a bedtime ritual that will help her switch gears. She might drink milk before bed, read something escapist, take a relaxing bath or hot shower, or place a hot water bottle or heating pad on her lower back or stomach. The important thing is using the same approach consistently, and it works best if bedtime happens at a fairly regular time. If this doesn't help, she should consider professional help.

SHE CAN'T FOCUS ON SCHOOLWORK. HOW CAN I HELP?

Most of us have problems focusing on work when we are tired, upset, in pain, feeling down, or focused on something else. This is compounded when someone suffers from depression. Both getting into gear and switching gears can be a real problem. She may have to re-learn how to focus and refocus. You might help by encouraging her to perform tasks in smaller bites, or by setting up a reward system. She can tell herself, "As soon as I finish this, I can make a phone call."

She may need to work on something while you're there. When children are small, they often engage in parallel play. They play side by side, doing different things, but they are aware of each other and enjoy each other's company. Try "parallel work." You bring your paperwork, she brings hers. Sit at the same table chipping away at your work and look up at each other from time to time and smile. Plan a snack break for an hour into it or meet at a coffee shop in off hours and spend a couple of hours working there.

The key is to break the inertia and get her moving. This momentum will carry her for a while, at least that same day, and she'll make inroads into her work. She may feel better about herself, too, and may be willing to try it again because it worked this time.

SHE JUST SITS AND STARES INTO SPACE. SHOULD I INTERRUPT HER OR LEAVE HER ALONE?

The best thing you can do for her is to join her. Sit for a while and say hello. Be content not to say anything for a while. Being there changes things because a part of her knows you are there. If you are relaxed, you'll communicate that to her. Just wait, or look up from time to time and smile. If ten, fifteen minutes pass, you might make a suggestion and see if you get a response. Make sure you use her name when you talk to her.

You can say:

- "I'm going to turn on some music. I think it would be nice. I hope you don't mind."
- "I'm a little thirsty all of a sudden. I'm going to get a drink. Can I get you one?"
- "I see a magazine lying on the table. I think I'll pick it up and take a look at it."
- "I need to stretch my legs. I think I'll take a walk around the block. Would you like to join me?"
- "I need some fresh air. Is there anywhere you'd like to go today?"

HE WON'T TALK TO ME. HOW CAN I HELP HIM IF HE JUST GRUNTS AND GETS ANGRY IF I PRESS FOR MORE?

Instead of asking questions about his situation or how he feels, tell him about *your* situation and how *you* feel. Tell him a funny story from work. Tell him about a problem you can't solve. Tell him a joke. Ask if he'd rather you didn't talk, or would rather have silence. If he'd rather you didn't talk, tell him you'd like to stick around for a while, "no pressure." Sip a cup of coffee, read a book or magazine, close your eyes for a few minutes.

Try to take your lead from him.

SHE CRIES ALL THE TIME. WHAT CAN I DO TO HELP?

This could indicate severe depression, so the best person to help her is a trained professional. In the meantime, you can be there to provide encouragement and comfort.

If she tells you she cries all the time, remind her of how strong she is the rest of the day.

- "It's no wonder you cry a lot; I would, too. The amazing thing is that you don't cry all the time."
- "You are so strong. I don't know how you manage all the things you do."
- "I couldn't handle things this well; you are incredible."

If she starts crying when you are there, hug her and say:

- "Would you like me to stay with you?"
- "You are so strong; I'd be crying all the time."
- "This is very, very hard."
- "I think you are a wonderful person. I want you to know that."

WHAT IF SHE WON'T EAT?

People who are depressed tend to lose interest in everything, including food, which may seem gray and unpalatable. But there are a number of ways to lose one's appetite. Pain and stress could be causing nausea, irritable bowel syndrome, ulcers, heartburn—any of which could suppress the appetite. She may not have the will or the energy to cook, or she may associate cooking with what once were positive things and now just remind her of her losses, or she may be accustomed to eating with other people and now that the depression has led her to withdraw and isolate herself, food just isn't appetizing.

Offer to cook for her. Invite her over to dinner or bring meal-sized portions to her house. Try meeting in a neutral place, such as a restaurant with no associations, and see if it makes a difference.

If she is losing weight, ask her about it. Let her know that you are worried and ask her if she's changed her eating habits. Ask her whether food appeals to her and, if not, why not. If she hasn't changed her eating habits, and says she still likes food, suggest she talk to her doctor.

Don't rule out the possibility of an eating disorder. They can be a way to regain control over one's life, so a person suffering from depression is particularly vulnerable to them. If you suspect this, it's okay to come right out and ask her about it. Both teenagers and mature adults can develop eating disorders, as can both men and women.

WHAT IF HE CAN'T SEEM TO STOP EATING?

Depression can lead to undereating or overeating. If he overeats, it is probably because food brings him comfort, keeps his mouth and hands busy, and is something he can still enjoy. The very act of eating—smelling the food, seeing the presentation, cutting it up—all carry positive associations of family dinners and celebrations and holidays. We talk about eating certain foods at certain times as eating "soul food." For someone suffering from depression, that phrase may no longer be figurative. Lack of sleep may contribute to overeating, too, since energy has to come from somewhere.

Depending on his weight to start with and any dietary restrictions he may already have had, there may be room for a little temporary weight gain. Unless his health is threatened, don't make an issue of the overeating. Instead provide other activities that require his full attention or the use of his hands. When our hands are fully engaged in something else, we are less likely to eat.

WHAT SHOULD I DO IF HE IS ANGRY ALL THE TIME?

When depression takes the form of anger, it may be harder on you but it makes things easier on the person who is depressed. When he is angry, he may feel as if he is about to explode, but at least he doesn't feel as if he is dissolving into nothingness. Anger is energy, and that may be something he hasn't felt coursing through him in a long time. Sometimes that anger can be channeled into positive action: telling someone how awful it is, writing a letter, making changes for the better.

Of course, it can be negative, too. It can be destructive to himself or someone else. It can be turned inward or can result in passionate acts of the moment she will regret later on. If her rage seems dangerous or you think he might hurt someone, call his therapist or an intervention center and let them know.

But more often, expressing her anger will help her, so don't get angry back. You will only fuel it. Don't tell her not to be angry; she has a right to her anger. Don't tell her that anger won't help; she knows that it won't help the situation, but it can provide temporary relief and, in any case, just now she can't help it. If you say either of these things, you may end up fueling her anger, and having it directed at you. And even worse, if you take away anger, she may collapse into desolation and shrink into herself in pain. Anger is a way of breaking out of it; don't take that away from her.

And don't tell her not to take it out on you; it's not personal, venting may help, and she's likely to apologize when she stops. She needs a place to vent and a person to vent to. Choosing you is a testament to your relationship and her trust in you.

How can you respond? By getting angry *for* her. Tell her you are angry that this is happening to her and angry that you can't change it.

When she has calmed down, you can help her by talking it over with her. Help her figure out why she is angry and find out what she'd like you to do when it happens again. Try to pinpoint what is triggering her outbursts and what you can do to avoid them.

Part VI

KIDS AND TEENAGERS

*"A moment's insight
is sometimes worth a life's experience."*

OLIVER WENDELL HOLMES SR.

Chapter Sixteen

Tips for Kids

When Someone in the Family Is Suffering from Depression

When children have someone in their lives who is struggling with depression, they may not know what is wrong, but they know something is different, and it often causes them to suffer. We, the adults in their lives, need to help them understand what is going on, answer their questions, provide reassurance, and help them cope.

When discussing someone in their lives who is depressed, what you tell them about depression and how long it lasts will depend on how mature they are and how much they want to know. If the child is older, you can share a lot of what is in the rest of this book with him.

This section discusses how to talk to a child about depression. This chapter focuses on what the depression of someone close to him means; the next chapter will help you talk to a child who is depressed himself. This chapter is presented in question-and-answer format to bring up questions a child might have and suggest ways to answer them.

The best way to reassure a child is to let her know that you are being straightforward and honest. Knowing you are there for her and that she can trust you will make the situation less scary.

HOW DO I ACT AROUND A DEPRESSED PERSON?

The average kid can continue to act like he usually does: not terribly solicitous, not angry or demanding, not totally ignoring the person who is sick. A kid's normalcy around a person suffering from depression will promote more normal functioning. People put out a special effort for kids, and not just for their own kids.

So kids should talk about the same things they usually talk about—friends, school, games, a good book, what's been exciting lately, what's been boring. They can ask for advice, offer a hug, write a special note or card, share a treat they were given, or pass on a joke.

Laughter is important, so you can suggest renting a video they would both think is funny, and encourage the child to tell a funny story that happened to him. But explain to kids that the usual ways of cheering people up may not always work, or that they might not see the usual results, smiles and laughter. The reaching out will help, though. Make sure the child knows this.

IS DEPRESSION CONTAGIOUS?

If they ask this, reassure them that it's not something you catch from someone else. Explain that just because someone in the family is struggling with it doesn't mean the children are going to get it, too, even if it makes them sad to see the person depressed.

If they are older, and the depression actually runs in the family, you may want to discuss that with them, but be careful because this could overload them emotionally. However, if they specifically ask if this could happen to them when they grow up, or if they are about to go off to college or live apart from you, have the conversation. For the kids going off to live on their own—which is very stressful because there are so many new things to deal with—you might want to talk a little about self-awareness.

Be matter-of-fact and point out that depression is not something you inherit such as brown hair or green eyes, but is a genetic predisposition. If they inherited the predisposition, it doesn't mean they'll certainly develop depression, it just means they have a greater chance of getting it than someone without the genetic predisposition would. On the other hand, many people with genetic predispositions never end up getting the illness—whether the predisposition is for depression, cancer, heart attacks, or diabetes. They should also keep in mind that science is always advancing in knowledge and with treatments.

WHAT ABOUT ME?

If a parent is suffering from depression, there may well be an atmosphere of doom and gloom in their home quite a lot of the time. The other parent may be stressed out and exhausted and therefore have little patience and less time to give to family members who are not depressed. Maybe they won't be able to go over homework all the time, or drive children to their activities. If the family member with depression is an adult and can't manage going to work, there could be less money, too, for clothes, cars, even going out to a movie or dinner once in a while.

Try to remember to ask your children what would help *them*. They need to know that all the focus in the family hasn't shifted to the person who is depressed, that they are still important. Make a point of telling children that you might get grumpy because you're tired, and that it won't be because you're upset with them. Consult them on what they think would help. Ask them what they absolutely have to get a ride to and what they can skip. If some of this is what Dad usually does, let them know that you know you're just a substitute, and maybe not a very good one in this area, but that they are not going to be left without support.

IS SHE GOING TO GET BETTER?

This is the toughest question you must be prepared to face because you don't know the answer. If it's true, you could say, "She gets better all the time, better than she was the day before." Or you can say that most people can be effectively treated, and that we're going to keep trying to help until it works. But it's important that you be truthful.

Don't guess, or wish, or pronounce some likely date when the person will get better. Tell her that you don't know. It varies from person to person. If pressed, say it can range anywhere from a few weeks to a few months to years, and the best thing all of you can do is take one day at time. But don't leave children with too much uncertainty, or a feeling that everything is spinning out of control. Let them know you have a plan. That Dad is seeing a doctor who is experienced in helping people with depression and he's taking medicine or working with the doctor so he can get better.

WHOSE FAULT IS IT?

You need to explain that it's not the person's fault, that he didn't bring it on himself. Explain that there are many possible causes of depression and that doctors don't always know exactly why it happens.

You also need to stress that it is not the child's fault. This is particularly important for young children who might not talk about what's happening or ask questions. They still notice what is happening, but they tend to interpret it in terms of themselves. They are often scared because they don't understand it and they are angry because they are not getting the attention they are used to getting. And, unless they are very young, they feel guilty about being angry.

How can I help?

Just as children need to learn to be compassionate and patient when someone is sick, so do they need to be these things for the person suffering from depression. This is something older children might do automatically. (This can be hard for teens, though, as this is a time when so many things are happening in their lives that they can't help but be very busy and self-absorbed.)

Make your children participants. Don't isolate them from family life or the person who is depressed. They can be part of the caring network; they can make a difference. Recognizing that strengthens them and the entire family.

"We are able to laugh when we achieve detachment, if only for a moment."

✸ MAY SARTON

Chapter Seventeen

Tips About Kids

WHEN THEY ARE DEPRESSED THEMSELVES

*I*t may not always look the same, but kids can suffer from the same forms of depression that adults do. If an adult is suffering from depression, it is possible that a child in the family may develop depression also. So, though the focus of this book is how to support the adults in your lives, learning a little bit about childhood depression might be helpful. If you are aware of what it looks like, you will be more likely to recognize it and get the child help.

WHAT DOES IT LOOK LIKE?

The main thing to look for is a number of changes in behavior, which could happen all of a sudden or gradually over a period of months. You can't count on a child to tell you that something's wrong, or to say he is very sad, or to tell you that life has no meaning to her. And if you ask, you are likely to get short answers that push you away: "Nothing's wrong" or "Leave me alone."

SOME SYMPTOMS OF CHILDHOOD DEPRESSION:

- Irritability
- All new friends, no more old friends
- Not having friends over or going to their homes
- Not wanting to do anything or always wanting to be out somewhere
- Change in appetite
- Oversleeping, inability to sleep, or taking lots of naps
- Schoolwork is not getting done or is suddenly done poorly
- Concern from teachers
- Acting out a lot
- Hyper all the time or quiet all the time
- Secretive
- Getting in trouble
- Alcohol or drugs

Significant changes in their lives such as a divorce, a move, a death or intense new conflict in the family may trigger some of these behaviors for a while, but that wouldn't necessarily mean they suffer from clinical depression. However, if these symptoms go on for a number of months and don't seem to be lessening at all, their reaction may have turned into depression.

HOW CAN ADULTS HELP?

If you suspect depression, it would be a good idea to get the child a medical checkup. This could uncover that something else is wrong, or rule out physical causes and be the first step in getting treatment for depression. In addition, kids will sometimes tell a doctor something they won't tell their parents. This is more likely to happen if the parent isn't in the examining room and if the child is school-age.

If you are the parent, you might want to let the doctor know about your concerns ahead of time. Explain that you are seeing these specific changes and you would appreciate an evaluation. If the doctor thinks it might be depression, she may handle treatment herself or she may refer your child to someone else for evaluation and/or treatment.

How kids view the world

Whether you are the parent or another adult in that child's life, you will want to provide him with all the caring and support you can so he can get through this strong and whole. This book can help you, but keep in mind that children and teens experience the world differently than you do because they are still developing. They see things differently and they think differently. They differ in how they process deep emotion and in their ability to express it. When talking to childhood depression, try to remember what it was like to be a kid.

Adults develop a deeper capacity for pain as they grow through life, and it can be all-encompassing. Adults also have the benefit of experience. They know they have gotten through difficult times and impossible emotions before, and they have a chance at believing that this will be doable now. In many cases, they also have the advantage of being responsible for someone else besides themselves so they can force themselves to function at some level. They will often hang on so that their children won't suffer pain or guilt or shame.

But kids don't have a sense of having weathered storms before, or of having developed skills and coping mechanisms for the bad times. And that is why depression is so devastating for the young. They don't know time passes or that they catch up with it. To kids, time drags on forever. Especially painful or boring times. And they don't know that they are not unique. They feel this has never happened to anyone else before, that no one in the entire world can relate to what is happening to them, and that there is no way out. Nor do they have that incredible feeling of love and caring for a child of their own to help them hang on—that sense of being needed in a special and irreplaceable way.

Kids are also impulsive and tend to act spontaneously without taking time to think. They don't wait to see if the impulse will fade and they are very susceptible to suggestion from their peers. This puts them at greater risk for dangerous behavior and for considering and then acting on suicidal thoughts. And something that looks like courting accidents might actually be deliberate. If you see self-destructive behavior in a child, don't be afraid to come right out and ask him if he is trying to hurt himself.

On the other hand, kids have more resilience, energy, and zest for life. They are better at bouncing back because they haven't been bounced quite as often. They have the ability to put things behind them in general, or put things to the side and immerse themselves in the now. This means offering a suitable distraction can help; it could be a friend, an activity, a vacation.

Talk to children and let them know you are trying to understand what they are going through. And if they don't believe you've ever had similar experiences yourself, just be there to listen.

A SPECIAL GROUP—TEENS

Teenagers are the toughest group to support. They are dealing with shifting hormones, messages from the media, fitting in with a peer group, changing relationships with the opposite sex, trying to decide who they are and who they want to be. In addition, teenagers are busy with the job of separating from their parents. This means they are less likely to ask for help or listen to what parents have to say. Teenagers are also dealing with the conviction that they are becoming adults, with the physical maturity, strength, and infallibility they'd like to associate with that accomplishment.

With teenagers, a certain amount of moodiness is to be expected. But if the bad mood never seems to lift and they exhibit the symptoms of depression listed in the FAQ section, they may be falling into depression.

If this is the case, the best thing you can do for them is to let them know you are available to listen, to talk, and to spend time with them. Get them evaluated for depression, and if necessary get them the appropriate treatment and make sure that they are sticking with it. Answer their questions and show them the same respect you show adults.

Keep in mind that an unwillingness to accept help and an inability to follow through on suggestions aren't just part of being a teenager, they are also symptoms of depression. This doesn't just make it difficult for parents to recognize that their kids are suffering from depression, it makes it that much harder for teenagers to struggle through it and for the adults around them to help.

There is a lot for teens and adults who love them to contend with all at once. Like adults with depression, teens can be silent and withdrawn, or consumed with rage, but in addition they can be sullen and uncooperative. As with adults, depression can impair judgment, but so can some of the things teens experiment with, such as drugs and alcohol.

One of the ways you can help is to make sure they hear positive messages about themselves. Tell them. Show them. Let them overhear you tell other people, and be specific. Tell him how proud you are of him for performing a particular action. Tell her you noticed something she said or did that shows how much character and integrity she has. Tell him how struck you are by something he said, and how clear it is to you that he is kind and empathetic, and that you have enormous respect for the person he is. Tell her it took enormous inner strength to make the decision she made and to carry it out. Tell him that even though he is not a grown man yet, in this he acted like a man. Tell her that you always knew she would be a daughter to be proud of.

Teens are dealing with so much, and trying to do everything on their own. They may think that it is up to them to deal with depression on their own, too. They might not be willing to accept the diagnosis, either. Be aware that teens might need to recover from the "idea" that they suffer from depression. It might make them feel like they don't fit in anymore.

They may ask what is happening and why it is happening. Explain it at a level they can grasp, but don't sugarcoat what's going on, and make sure they don't think it's their fault.

If their depression is biologically based, be prepared to help them recover from this information. Teens, especially, haven't quite figured out who they are and this can really shake their sense of self. Make sure they understand this is a part of them, but not who they are, and that it is not intrinsic to who they are any more than asthma would be, or diabetes, or a food allergy. Help them regain a sense of confidence in themselves, and give them time to do this.

Friends and parents are a major part of the recovery process because they are a part of the nonclinical world, the world the teens aren't sure they fit in anymore. The world that represents ordinary hopes and challenges, fun and friendships. Other adults who believe in them are also very important. Often, when teens are focusing on separating from their parents, relationships with other adults who can listen, go on outings, mentor them, and make them feel like an almost peer will be of enormous help.

Some of this will still apply to young people as they enter their twenties and go off on their own. This group faces enormous challenges and can be overwhelmed with stress and decision making: completing college, entering professional training programs, starting their first full-time jobs, launching careers, living on their own, becoming responsible for living expenses, managing a budget, entering into significant relationships and new marriages, and becoming parents. All this takes place while they may still be completing their separation from their parents and becoming fully adult. They, too, can develop depression and you, as their parents, will want to be there for them.

SOME THINGS TO SAY:

- "We're going to get through this. Just hold on to me."
- "Don't look so far ahead. Let's get through a few minutes at a time."
- "There might not be any shortcuts through this, but there are 'long' cuts. Not following a treatment plan is a long cut."
- "I'm really proud of you for the way you are handling this. It's one of the toughest things there is to do."
- "You've got guts. I'm proud to be your mother/father."
- "This isn't going to be easy, and I guess you noticed that already. But we can do this together."
- "You're a great kid. This doesn't change that. If anything, I'm prouder of you than ever."
- "I know you are doing the best you can."

- "I know this takes a lot of energy. It's a pretty big fight, isn't it? I'd be tired, too."
- "You know what? You have good friends because you are a good friend."
- "Hey, this is scary for you, right? It's not surprising it's scary for some of your friends. Or maybe they just don't know what to say. You could tell them that, you know—just tell them they don't have to say anything special. Just act the way they usually do."

Part VII

Taking Care of Yourself

"The mind, like nature, abhors a vacuum."

❧ VICTOR HUGO

Chapter Eighteen

Talking to Yourself

SUSTAINING YOUR STRENGTH

*D*epression doesn't just take a toll on the people struggling with it, it takes a toll on the people who care about them and it puts them at risk for developing depression themselves. Not because depression is contagious—it isn't—but because unremitting stress can trigger depression. This can happen if you live with someone who has severe depression and you have made helping him a primary part of your life.

This section explores ways to tell if you are becoming depressed and what steps to take if you are. Fortunately, there are a number of simple ways to reduce stress before it can turn into depression. This section also includes examples of these stress-reducing activities and ways to put them into action. They are all commonsense methods, but when we are stressed and overwhelmed, it is easy to forget about them.

PAYING ATTENTION TO YOUR HEALTH

It isn't always easy to see the signs of depression in yourself. If you feel exhausted, it is probably because of all the extra demands on your physical time and your emotional space. And if you no longer feel like doing anything pleasurable, it might be because all you want to do is catch up on chores, work, commitments, and sleep. But if you find you can't think of anything you'd enjoy doing, or even remember what you used to enjoy doing, you may be developing depression. If this is the case, do an inventory of other signs of depression to see if you have any more.

If your friends and family express concern, say you never make time for them or for yourself, and that they're worried about you, listen to them. It's a wake-up call.

If you start slipping at work, things start falling between the cracks, the people you work with are getting frustrated or expressing concern, stop to take a breath. Step back and assess yourself.

WHAT TO DO IF YOU START TO SHOW SIGNS OF DEPRESSION

If you think you are sliding into depression, take steps right away so you can stop it in a mild stage. Don't wait for it to become full-blown. Do the same things you would do for the person you care about that you already are doing for them. Get a depression screening, consult a doctor, and enlist the help of family and friends. This is a very tough disease to conquer single-handedly. It may be the hardest lesson you have to learn, but don't be embarrassed to ask for help. Spend time with friends and accept their support. This is not a time to be alone.

TAKING CARE OF YOURSELF

Managing stress can help you avoid developing depression in the first place. You may think, "There's nothing I can do about that now. I can't take the time or the energy. My needs will come later." But you could crash, too. You need to be healthy—physically and mentally and emotionally—for both your sakes, and you need to find ways to stay healthy even though there seems to be no spare time at all in your days.

Your frame of mind can make a big difference. Accept that you can't do everything, that you can't be all things, that you need nourishment, too. If you can realize this, something will relax inside and you will feel you are able to breathe.

The rest of this section is devoted to stress-management techniques that can help ward off depression and give you energy to support the people you care about.

SLOW DOWN

Slowing down your breathing or your walking pace doesn't just slow down your body rhythms, it slows down your mind. All that rushing around we tend to do, whether in the kitchen or in the car or at work, doesn't tend to save more than a couple of minutes anyway. It only feels as if it does. (Try measuring it sometime.) But it certainly adds to our tension.

Take time to savor the positive in your life: moments, textures, visual displays, sounds, aromas, tastes. And these don't take time. A minute here, three seconds there. If they add up to ten or twenty minutes a day, the world won't tip off its axis. When you can live in the moment and appreciate what *is*, not only will you relax but you will get more enjoyment out of life.

TREAT YOURSELF

One way to take care of yourself is to treat yourself to something every day, and that doesn't mean spending money. Exercise a little, talk to a friend, take a nap, accomplish a personal or household task. Of course, shopping is okay, too!

If you're doing a lot around the house and working full-time, providing support to the person suffering from depression, you need to add these things back to your life.

Little changes add cheer, shift perspective a little, awaken senses, help you see things differently. They can also reenergize and relax you, and get you out of your rut.

Ten-minute treats:
- daydream a vacation
- take a bubble bath
- sit outside in the sun
- walk around the block
- lean back in a favorite chair and close your eyes for ten minutes
- eat a piece of fruit
- dunk something sweet in a cup of coffee
- make a long-distance call to someone who loves you
- buy flowers for the table
- read a chapter in a book you like
- take a long, luxurious shower
- light a candle and enjoy its glow for ten minutes
- get a foot massage
- throw together an exotic drink (with your blender), and sip it slowly
- play a favorite song
- pull out a musical instrument and reacquaint yourself with it
- dance with an invisible partner

- cook your favorite food
- put a spice you love in boiling water so you can breathe it in
- lie down with cucumber slices on your eyes

CHANGE YOUR ROUTINE

You might be surprised at how many ruts you're in and the dulling effect they have on your senses. Getting out of the *big one* is hard and it takes a long time—whether it is your depression or the depression of someone you care about. But there are little ones you can work on that will have an effect that will surprise you. You can do this by changing the things you don't usually think about. Little changes help pave the way for bigger ones and make it easier to get out of a negative state of mind.

Some small changes you can make:
- You probably sit at the same seat at every meal. Change it.
- You probably use the same size, brand, color of paper napkins. Go wild and crazy or sweet and sentimental. Pick something silly. But, every few weeks, change them!
- After dinner, you probably have a favorite chair you sit in, or a particular part of the couch. Sit somewhere else.
- Mix and match your wardrobe in a different way. Get a new piece of clothing or accessory that you normally wouldn't wear.
- Have an office? See if you can rearrange it.
- Are there childhood dishes you haven't eaten in a long time? Make one for your family.
- Buy a new wastepaper basket, change cleansers, try a different scent, use a different trash bag.

- Change your exercise routine. Try a new type of exercises, vary the order in which you do them, do them in a different place, wear different clothes while you do them.
- Replace a plant you feel blah about and get one you enjoy looking at.

WORTHWHILE ACTIVITIES

There are a number of ways to structure your day, but the key is to find activities that mean something to you or have worthwhile results. Sometimes we get stressed and overwhelmed because we have no time to relax, but other times it is because we aren't doing work that feels productive, creative or enriching.

The mind insists on being filled. But new thoughts can push out old thoughts, or at least force them to the side. Make that work for you by including components in your day that not only set it up, but give you a sense of accomplishment at the end of the day.

Some activities include:
- If you don't have a job, get one, even if it's volunteer work. Fill up time (and your mind) with it. It might provide a distraction, a respite, and healing.
- Reach out to others. Call people to see how they are, to say hello, to tell them they did a good job on something, or how much you appreciate them.
- Volunteer your time to a cause you care about in your community. It doesn't have to be time-consuming or frequent, but it's a way to have regular contact with other people and to work on something that doesn't have to have anything to do with the other parts of your life.
- Find a hobby if you don't already have one, or go back to

one you've set aside. Start a collection, paint, write, join a team, work on a family tree.

- Learn something new by taking a class, using software, reading a book, or from someone you know. Filling your mind with something new will give you an ongoing sense of accomplishment, and will distract you from negative thoughts.
- Follow an old dream you never had time for. What do you have to lose? Be a child rummaging in the attic and trying on the clothes she finds there. Rummage through your dreams and see how they fit.
- Do something that involves living things and growing. Plant a garden, set a pot of herbs on your kitchen windowsill, start an avocado pit, get a "mini-tomato" plant, start a cactus collection, get a fish, turtle, or bird.
- Cleaning is satisfying, especially if you can see the dirt either before you clean or on the rag you are using. Throwing things away, reorganizing, or straightening out also helps with mental cleansing . . . and it's creative. You are making things fresh, new, different.
- Go outside and breathe or sit in the sun. Even if it's cold outside, poke your nose out for sixty seconds and breathe in the fresh air.
- Exercising gets the oxygen moving and the serotonin pumping. It helps you focus on your body instead of your mind and it helps body and mind reharmonize.

START SMALL.

Add worthwhile activities to your life a couple at a time. You may have to force yourself to do this at first, and it might be difficult to do this consistently, day in and day out. But after a few weeks, it'll get easier, and once it's a habit, you can start adding more.

When you are suffering from depression it is important to set specific goals. In the first week, try to do something for yourself each day (maybe a treat). In the second week try to do three things for yourself each day (maybe a treat, a household task, or calling a friend). Doing these things will push negative feelings into the background and help you stay connected to yourself.

Afterword

Easing the Way

*T*his book is not only about easing the way for the people in your life who suffer from depression; it is also about easing your way as you offer them support. Please keep in mind that the suggestions in this book about what to say and what not to say are just that—suggestions. Every situation is different and will require you to adjust the form your words take. But the reason behind them is always to bring dignity and compassion to a loved one's life and make strength seem possible.

We all need to experience joy, to let ourselves hope, to believe in possibilities. These are things someone suffering from depression has lost. We can't give those back, but we can help sustain those things that provide a foundation for them: connection to other people, self-respect, and a sense of purpose.

When we adjust a kaleidoscope slightly, patterns can shift and colors can dazzle. With subtle changes in what we say and do, we can help relieve the unrelenting gray of their world. That's what we want to help them with. We want to bring the color back, bring the energy back, bring the person back.

Life should be about holding and being held, not just about holding on. It is my hope that this book will help you do that, and that in the process you will find or rediscover parts of you that were silent. In the giving is the receiving.

Wishing all of you well.

Resources

WHERE TO FIND OUT MORE

Many people have faced what you are facing now, either because they have suffered with someone they care about or because they have struggled with depression themselves. And many of them have taken steps to help those who come after them. They have written books, formed organizations, started Web sites, launched newsletters and magazines, and created support groups.

They can help you find a support group in your area, and they can help with specific information on depression types, severity, treatments, and side effects, as well as with issues such as insurance, current research, and the law.

When researching these organizations, I found that the people on staff went out of their way to be helpful.

Here's how to find them.

NOTE: The focus here is on resources that will help *you* support friends and family members.

ORGANIZATIONS

Depression and Bipolar Support Alliance (DBSA)
(formerly known as the National Depressive and
Manic-Depressive Association) Chicago, Illinois

DBSA focuses on providing support. It is a national network of support groups with resources, information, online forums, and a bookstore. There is a wide selection of free informational materials for both the people struggling with depression and their families. It also provides online confidential screening for bipolar disorder and referrals to other sources of help. You can reach someone by phone weekdays, 8:30 A.M. to 5:00 P.M., CST, for informational materials or a referral to a local support group. Voice-mail messages left at other times are responded to the next business day. E-mail is returned promptly.

Depression and Related Affective Disorders Association (DRADA)
Baltimore, Maryland

Affiliated with Johns Hopkins School of Medicine, this organization is a partnership of consumers, family members and mental-health professionals. It produces a quarterly newsletter—*Smooth Sailing*—as well as helpful books and videos for adults, teens, and children. It offers cutting-edge research information, an extensive network of support groups in the Baltimore-Washington area and the surrounding region—including Maryland, Virginia, Delaware and southeastern Pennsylvania—and provides training for support group leaders. Call to find a support group near you, or for other information or materials. The phone is manned by volunteers, and you will generally be able to reach someone between 9:00 A.M. and 3:00 P.M. on weekdays. A message can be left at any time, 24/7, and someone will get back to you within two days.

National Mental Health Association
Alexandria, Virginia

This is a broad spectrum organization that provides information and support, and lobbies for research funds for all kinds of mental illnesses, for legislation that helps people with mental illnesses (in the way they are helped with physical ones), and for other mental-health issues. NMHA focuses on public education on mental health as well as on mental illness. There are 340 affiliates nationwide. When you call, you will reach a resource specialist who can talk to you about your concerns and refer you to local support services. And there is an option to reach a Spanish-speaking resource specialist as well. NMHA also has informational materials it can send you; they normally do this within forty-eight hours. Their specialists are available 9:00 A.M. to 5:00 P.M., weekdays, EST. You can leave a voice-mail message days, nights, and weekends, or communicate via e-mail; if you leave a message, someone will get back to you within two business days.

NMHA doesn't focus on depression but is one of the founding sponsors of **National Depression Screening Day,** which is now run by Mental Health Inc. each October. If you suspect depression and the person you care about won't talk about it or see a doctor, you might be able to have him do this. The screening is confidential, totally anonymous, and free. And it only takes ten to twenty minutes. It is performed by mental-health professionals in towns and cities throughout the country. So if he is uncomfortable about running into someone he knows, he can go to a screening site in another city. If the screening suggests depression is present, the mental-health professional will provide refer-rals, and then the person you care about can follow up. "Dear Annie" (formerly the Ann Landers column) typically devotes her column to this a few weeks beforehand and provides an 800 number so people can find a screening site near them. In 1999, there were 3,000 such sites across the country. In 2002 there were 6,307 sites; 256,754 people at-tended the event and 126,132 people chose to do the screening. For more information, the Web site is www.mentalhealthscreening.org.

Child and Adolescent Bipolar Foundation (CABF)
Wilmette, Illinois

CABF is an organization of parents that provides support through an online community of parents, medical professionals, mental-health professionals, researchers, scientists, and educators. It is a source of support and information and advocacy, raising awareness of bipolar disorder in children and helping parents work with school systems to give children the best environment and appropriate ac-commodations so that they can not just cope but thrive. It also has a database of doctors built on referrals from satisfied parents. The Web site (www.bpkids.org) provides e-mail addresses for key staff mem-bers and team leaders. (Go to the Web site, select "Front Desk," then click on "About CABF.") Voice messages can be left at the main phone number, and callers can specify whether they want to speak to a staff member or a member of the organization's Family Response Team. Office hours are 8:00 A.M. to 5:00 P.M. EST. Voice messages can be left at any time and are generally returned within a day; e-mail is responded to promptly.

WEB SITES

www.nimh.nih.gov/publicat/depressionmenu.cfm
The National Institute of Mental Health provides brochures in English and Spanish. They can be downloaded or you can order a free copy.

www.depression-screening.org
This site provides a wealth of general information, first-person accounts, and links to other resources. It is also a confidential screening site, helping you determine whether you or someone you care about is suffering from depression. This is a year-round depression screening site available online.

www.dougy.org
www.grievingchild.org
help@dougy.org
This is an online resource for grieving kids, teens, and the people who care about them. Its purpose is to help children deal with their grief after the death of someone close to them. It is a service of the Dougy Center and is supported by private funding. It provides age-appropriate information to kids, teens, and adults, refers them to local centers where they can find support and give support to others struggling with the same pain, and points the way to other resources. Though the physical center is based in Portland, Oregon, its pioneering peer group support group concept has been brought to local communities throughout the country. The Dougy Center has provided training for centers throughout the United States and in a number of other countries. Each center is a safe place where children and teens can find peer support to help them through the grieving process. Each center is a safe place, a healing place, and the services are free. (You can also

write to The Dougy Center for Grieving Children, PO Box 86852, Portland, OR 97286, or call 503-775-5683 for more information.)

FROM THE INSIDE: VOICES OF THOSE WHO HAVE SUFFERED FROM DEPRESSION

These people have come out the other side. They have lived to tell about it, even when they have suffered recurrences, even when they anticipate another bout coming on. They are a testament to what is possible: that there is another side, that there is hope.

Cronkite, Kathy. *On the Edge of Darkness: Conversations About Conquering Depression.* New York: Dell, 1994. Inspiring accounts from a wealth of well-known people.

Jamison, Kay Redfield. *An Unquiet Mind.* New York: Random House, 1997. A psychologist tells the story of her own struggle with bipolar disorder.

Manning, Martha. *Undercurrents: A Life Beneath the Surface.* San Francisco: HarperCollins, 1995. A clinical psychologist traces her own route through depression, sharing the pain, the humor, the compensating strategies, the loss of function, the recurrence, and the various treatments and their results.

Solomon, Andrew. *The Noonday Demon: An Atlas of Depression.* New York: Scribner, 2001. A writer writing about his own depression—part info, part perspective, part treatment, part memoir.

Styron, William. *Darkness Visible: A Memoir of Madness*. New York: Vintage Books, 1990. This little book has touched millions. This Pulitzer Prize–winning author talks about what it feels like, how one thinks about it, and how depression takes over one's thought processes.

A Patient's Perspective—Mike Wallace. Video interview with CBS correspondent Mike Wallace, who speaks about his own depression in an interview with Dr. J. Raymond DePaulo Jr. The interview took place at DRADA's Mood Disorders Research/Education Symposium at Johns Hopkins University School of Medicine in 1991. Produced by DRADA, 1992; 40 minutes; VHS. Can be obtained through DRADA, the Depression and Related Affective Disorders Association, in Baltimore, Maryland. Candid, disarming, funny and insightful comments by a man who single-handedly helped change the public's perception of depression. Men find this tape particularly accessible.

HELPFUL BOOKS IN GENERAL

Berger, Diane, and Lisa Berger. *We Heard the Angels of Madness: A Family Guide to Coping with Manic Depression*. New York: William Morrow & Co., 1992.

DePaulo, J. Raymond Jr., M.D., and Leslie Alan Horvitz. *Understanding Depression: What We Know and What You Can Do About It*. New York: John Wiley & Sons, 2002.

Pinsky, Drew, M.D., ed. *Restoring Intimacy: The Patient's Guide to Maintaining Relationships During Depression.* Baltimore, Md.: NDMDA, 1999. Both the depression itself and the treatment choice can affect a relationship. This book talks about how to recognize depression, how to cope with its effects, how to discuss issues with a doctor. ISBN 0-9673893-0-5. It can be ordered from DBSA (see "Resources—Organizations").

Rosenthal, Norman E., M.D. *Winter Blues: Seasonal Affective Disorder: What It Is and How to Overcome It.* New York: Guilford Publications, Inc., 1993.

Sheffield, Anne. *How You Can Survive When They're Depressed: Living and Coping with Depression Fallout.* New York: Crown, 1999.

HELPFUL BOOKS ON CHILDHOOD DEPRESSION

Cytryn, Leon, M.D., and Donald McKnew, M.D. *Growing Up Sad: Childhood Depression and Its Treatment.* New York: W. W. Norton, 1996.

Fassler, David G., M.D., and Lynne S. Dumas. *"Help Me, I'm Sad": Recognizing, Treating, and Preventing Childhood and Adolescent Depression.* New York: Penguin, 1997.

Ingersoll, Barbara D., Ph.D., and Sam Goldstein, Ph.D. *Lonely, Sad and Angry: A Parent's Guide to Depression in Children and Adolescents.* New York: Doubleday Books, 1995.

Papolos, Demitri, F. M.D., and Janice Papolos. *The Bipolar Child: The Definitive and Reassuring Guide to Childhood's Most Misunderstood Disorder.* Revised and Expanded Edition. New York: Broadway Books, 2002.

FOCUS ON TREATMENTS

Klein, Donald F., M.D., and Paul H. Wender, M.D. *Understanding Depression: A Guide to Its Diagnosis and Treatment.* New York: Oxford University Press, 1993. Focus on pharmacology.

Hammerly, Milton, M.D. *Depression: The New Integrative Approach: How to Combine the Best of Traditional and Alternative Therapies.* Avon, Mass.: The Philip Lief Group, Inc., Adams Media Corporation, 2001.

O'Connor, Richard, Ph.D. *Undoing Depression: What Therapy Doesn't Teach You and Medication Can't Give You.* New York: Berkley Books, 1997. Discusses various approaches one by one and how they work in combination. (Also describes ways to change habits of thinking that can make recovery more difficult and recurrence more likely.)

FOCUS ON SYMPTOMS

Day for Night: Recognizing Teenage Depression. A videotape produced by DRADA; 26 minutes; VHS. Can be obtained through DRADA, the Depression and Related Affective Disorders Association, in Baltimore, Maryland.

Papolos, Demitri, F. M.D., and Janice Papolos. *Overcoming Depression.* New York: HarperCollins, 1992. Third edition, 1997.

CONNECTING WITH SUPPORT GROUPS

For a national network of support groups, contact **DBSA** (Depression and Bipolar Support Alliance), in Chicago. They have an 800 number (800-826-3632) and will help you find a support group in your local area.

For an extensive regional network of support groups radiating from a hub in Baltimore, Maryland, and ranging over six states, contact **DRADA** (Depression and Related Affective Disorders Association), in either Baltimore or Washington, D.C.

Also contact your local Mental Health Association, a local hospital, or your doctor. Connect with support groups through hospice, through AARP, through churches, synagogues, mosques. Your local newspaper might help, too. Local newspapers often run weekly columns that list meeting times and places for a variety of support groups.

If you want something less formal, either for yourself or the person you care about, talk to people who know what you are talking about because they are living it, too, or have been there. They may have practical suggestions, or may be able to connect you with a buddy system, or set one up with you themselves—checkup calls, regular meeting times, etc. Don't go it alone. Knowing someone else is in it with you, someone you can call on, someone who will check in, will make the impossible feel possible.

There is an organization that straddles the fence between formal and informal support. It's called **Recovery, Inc.** and it's in a number of countries. It's a self-help group that helps participants manage their symptoms. This organization, which has been helping people for several generations, provides initial training and regular updates for its group leaders. Its approach is based on a medical research model for aftercare; its focus is to help people trade insecure thoughts for secure thoughts, defeatist thoughts for proactive thoughts. Examples of how meetings are run can be seen on the Web site (www.recovery-inc.com). Recovery, Inc. is intended to supplement professional care. Dear Abby has supported it in her column. Recovery, Inc.'s international headquarters is located in Chicago, Illinois.

And there is an organization that helps people with mood disorders and emotional challenges support each other. It is a twelve-step program run by laypeople, and it is open to people with all types of emotional difficulties, not just depression. This organization has groups all over the world. The organization is **Emotions Anonymous**, and it's based in St. Paul, Minnesota.

ESPECIALLY FOR KIDS

Dubuque, Nicholas, and Susan Dubuque. *Kid Power Tactics for Dealing with Depression*. New York: Childswork/Childsplay, 1996. Paperback. ISBN 1882732480. Aimed at kids in grades four through eight.

"Just a Mood . . . or Something Else?" A brochure for teens posted on the Web at http://dbsalliance.org. Point to "Programs and Publications," then click on "Brochures," scroll down and click on "Is It Just a Mood . . . or Something Else?"

FOR CUTTING-EDGE RESEARCH

This information will not help with the day-to-day aspects of relationships and support, but if you want to keep tabs on the latest ongoing research in neuroscience, this is a good place to start.

www.narsad.org
NARSAD is the largest funder of mental-health research outside of the U.S. government. You will find an online newsletter and information in both English and Spanish.

IF YOU HAVE LOST SOMEONE TO SUICIDE . . . OR FEAR YOU WILL

Here is a hotline plus six groups and three books to turn to:

National Suicide Hotline: 1-800-SUICIDE (800-784-2433)
The National Hopeline Network provides access to trained phone crisis workers seven days a week, twenty-four hours a day through this toll-free number. They are based in crisis centers across the country that have been certified by the American Association of Suicidology. The hotline is a service of the Kristin Brooks Hope Center (KBHC), which also provides other support and access to resources via its Web site (www.hopeline.com). KBHC is located in Purcellville, Virginia.

American Association of Suicidology (AAS)
Washington, District of Columbia

AAS is a national clearinghouse for information on suicide and promotes awareness, education, research, prevention and training. It publishes newsletters and a quarterly journal, refers people to survivor support groups, maintains a directory of helpful agencies, and is involved in the certification of crisis intervention centers and individuals working in the area of crisis management. Members include individuals, organizations, professionals in the field, and family members.

American Foundation for Suicide Prevention (AFSP)
New York, New York

AFSP supports research, training, education and public awareness, and connects people with support groups in their local communities. They publish a quarterly newsletter, *Lifesavers*, provide information and statistics, and are a source of useful programs. An example is their Teen Suicide Prevention Kits. They also run an annual National Survivor of Suicide Day (on the Saturday before Thanksgiving), which is broadcast by satellite to various centers across the country and available as a Webcast. This day creates a community of survivors who can connect to each other. People can register free on the Web site (www.afsp.org) and access the archives all year long.

Friends for Survival, Inc.
Sacramento, California

This is an organization that supports family members and friends who have lost someone to suicide. It is made up of people who have gone through this painful process themselves and want to help others who are facing it. They offer a Suicide Loss Helpline, a monthly newsletter, referrals to local sources of information and support, a Speakers Bureau to increase understanding in the community, and guidance and training in developing local chapters. The organization welcomes professionals as well as friends and family. It helps people deal with the many contradictory and painful emotions that come with grief and tragedy. The Suicide Loss Helpline is available to anyone who has been affected by a suicide, no matter how many days or years have gone by. Someone will respond within a day or two.

SAVE—Suicide Awareness/Voices of Education
Minneapolis, Minnesota
SAVE's mission is to educate the public about suicide prevention and to speak for suicide survivors. They are both a public-awareness group and a source of information. One of their programs is to provide teacher training in suicide prevention. Another is to provide Community Action Kits that people can use to get programs started in their own communities. Their newsletter—*Voices of SAVE*—can be read online. On a local level (within Minnesota), they also offer a Speakers Bureau. Voice-mail messages are generally responded to within forty-eight hours; e-mail is responded to promptly.

SOLOS—Survivors of Loved Ones' Suicides
Dumfries, Virginia
This is an interactive Web site (www.solos.org) that gives people a way to share their grief and reach out to others who are grieving. It contains memorial sites, a message board, a place to post tributes, and a variety of e-mail/chat support groups. It also refers people to helpful newsgroups and other resources. There are specialized support groups for different functions, such as facilitators of survivor support groups,

parents of attempters, and medical/crisis response teams. There are support groups based on relationships, such as parents, spouses, adult children, romantic partners, fathers, adult siblings, teens, kids, or grandparents. And there are support groups based on topics, such as postpartum suicide, murder-suicide, new survivors, and general discussion. Groups made up of teens have a moderator. Most chats have a host to keep intruders out. Groups in other languages will be formed as long as someone volunteers to lead them.

SPAN—Suicide Prevention Action Network
SPAN USA, Inc.
Marietta, Georgia

This site (www.spanusa.org) contains a wealth of material. It also provides many links to organizations, resources and helpful information. SPAN's mission is to prevent suicide; it is dedicated to developing strategies that work and to making suicide prevention a national priority. To accomplish this, it promotes awareness, develops grassroots campaigns, advocates for prevention funding, and supports local advocacy and prevention efforts.

Books:

Bolton, Iris, with Curtis Mitchell. *My Son . . . My Son: A Guide to Healing After a Suicide in the Family.* Roswell, Ga.: Bolton Press Atlanta, 1983 (revised).

Fine, Carla. *No Time to Say Goodbye: Surviving the Suicide of a Loved One.* New York: Main Street Books/Doubleday, 1999, © 1997.

Parkin, Rebecca, and Karen Dunne-Maxim. *Child Survivor of Suicide: A Guidebook for Those Who Care for Them*. Booklet. 1995. Available through AFSP, the American Foundation for Suicide Prevention (see above).